Wishing you many
spicy adventures!

Sam & Katie

the spice kitchen

the spice kitchen
everyday cooking with organic spices

SARA ENGRAM and KATIE LUBER with KIMBERLY TOQE

**Andrews McMeel
Publishing, LLC**
Kansas City · Sydney · London

FOR OUR FAMILIES—DIANA, JACOB, JOHN HENRY, PHIL, AND JACK—
WHO MAKE IT ALL WORTHWHILE.

09 10 11 12 13 WKT 10 9 8 7 6 5 4 3 2 1

Library of Congress Cataloging-in-Publication Data

Engram, Sara.
    The spice kitchen : everyday cooking with organic spices / Sara Engram & Katie Luber with Kimberly Toqe.
        p. cm.
    Includes bibliographical refrences and index.
    ISBN-13: 978-0-7407-7972-5
    ISBN-10: 0-7407-7972-9
    1. Cookery (Spices) 2. Spices. 3. Cookery (Natural foods) I. Luber, Katie. II. Toqe, Kimberly. III. Title.
    TX819.A1E65 2009
    641.3'383—dc22

                    2009006731

www.tspspices.com

www.andrewsmcmeel.com

Photography © David Morris Photography/www.davidmorrisphoto.com

Food styling by Kimberly Kissling and Tina Bell Stamos

Illustrations by Julie Pelaez

Book design by Julie Barnes

Book composition by Diane Marsh

ATTENTION: SCHOOLS AND BUSINESSES

Andrews McMeel books are available at quantity discounts with bulk purchase for educational, business, or sales promotional use. For information, please write to: Special Sales Department, Andrews McMeel Publishing, LLC, 1130 Walnut Street, Kansas City, Missouri 64106.

Acknowledgments

We have many people to thank for making this book a reality. Kimberly Toqe brought technical skill, imagination, and good humor to the task of pulling together and testing a collection of recipes that reflected our desire to help cooks broaden their use of spices in foods their families already know and love.

Anne Pushkal's formidable research skills, nimble writing, and infectious wit resulted in profiles of our favorite spices, herbs, and zests that will surely tempt even spice-shy cooks to expand their culinary horizons.

Many friends and colleagues helped us test and refine these recipes. Our thanks to Nancy Meadows, John Dearing, Stephanie Adler, Rosemary Connolly Gately, Amy Carey, Camille Peluso, Mary Leight, Adele Gammon, Lee Pierce, Edie Meacham, Grace Pollack, Pat Shaw, Jan Schroeder, and Edie Windsor for your suggestions, tests, and comments.

We extend our thanks to Lane Butler, Kirsty Melville, and all the helpful people at Andrews McMeel Publishing. You have been a pleasure to work with.

We are grateful to our families for putting up with all our spice experiments, and especially for their unwavering support as we have pursued our dream of spice enlightenment.

Tarragon and rosemary

Contents

Introduction

People like to change things. We turn dirt into dye, clay into cups, words into poems, and a grab bag of ingredients into meals as varied as a hearty wild-game cassoulet or a simple vegetable curry. This persistent urge to transform raw materials into something useful and appealing sets us apart from other creatures. Why settle for a plain slab of tough meat when you can season it, simmer it, and enjoy a feast?

In the annals of cooking, spices rank as one of our oldest and most reliable tools—right up there with fire and heat. Excavations of Neolithic caves have uncovered traces of cumin and other spices, evidence of an active spice trade reaching back 8,000 to 10,000 years—and prehistoric grounding for one of our favorite food mantras: eat locally, but season globally. Neolithic humans probably obtained their spices by way of trade routes established overland from India and Sri Lanka into Mesopotamia, the fertile "cradle of civilization," located between the Tigris and Euphrates rivers (now largely part of Iraq).

When archaeologists were able to decipher tablets dating back 4,000 years to the Mesopotamian empire of Babylon, they found records of numerous spices, including anise seed, cumin, coriander, mint, juniper, cardamom, fenugreek, mustard seed, and asafetida. Excavations of 4,000-year-old Mesopotamian archaeological sites have uncovered cloves far from their home in Indonesia.

The Babylonians even had recipe tablets with descriptions of more than 100 different varieties of soups and stews. In these recipes, meats were always braised in water with some form of fat and combinations of up to four spices—not so different from our "fusion" cooking of today.

The ancient Egyptians were spice lovers, too, cooking with cumin, anise, coriander, fenugreek, black mustard seed, fennel, dill, mint, marjoram, sage, and thyme. Spices also played a role in their elaborate death rituals. They were used in the mummification process, and the departed were always provided with a good supply of spices to accompany them into the afterlife. The Egyptians celebrated spices in life as well. On numerous occasions, the great pharaoh Ramses II presented cinnamon to the gods.

a word about organic spices

Some people believe organic certification for spices is less important than for other foods. We disagree. Spices, herbs, and zests provide concentrated flavors. When you taste a teaspoon of pure cinnamon or cumin or tarragon—with no fillers or additives or other substances—you get pure flavor, a real bang for your buck.

But because most spices are packaged in jars or bottles designed to hold as much as ¾ cup, they often need anti-caking agents or other additives. That dilutes the flavor, if only by a little bit. Moreover, regulations on herbs and spices are relatively loose, and those bargains—like that huge container of basil for a couple of dollars Sara kept in her cabinet for a decade—are likely to have a substantial amount of "filler." Organic spices must be pure, not diluted by fillers or additives.

Moreover, organic certification provides assurance that these ingredients do not contain pesticides. Organic certification is particularly important for zests, since pesticides used in growing nonorganic citrus fruits tend to lodge in the peel, providing an extra dose of toxins in nonorganic orange or lemon zest.

Around the world, spice growers and suppliers are recognizing that there is value in an organic designation. It tells consumers they get full value for their spice investment. Equally important, it creates working conditions that protect the health of workers and their families and encourages agricultural practices that sustain the environment in which spices and herbs grow best.

We think spices and herbs are among Nature's most magical gifts, gifts that we should treasure and relish. That's why we believe "organic" is important.

The Greeks and Romans followed suit, embracing a range of spices and herbs, including coriander (a favorite), cumin, cardamom, peppergrass, cress, saffron, and ginger grass. Cinnamon was a rare and beloved luxury—so costly that the Greek historian Herodotus suggested that it was secretly harvested from the nests of huge, dangerous birds in the mountains of Ethiopia.

The value the ancient Greeks ascribed to spices like cinnamon reflects a larger reverence for food and healthy living. By "diet," they meant a way of life that paid attention to the connections between sleeping and waking, exercise and rest, and, not least, food—consuming it, evacuating it, and all other factors that must be under control if a person is to be healthy, strong, and beautiful.

In light of today's food trends, it's worth noting that this Greek "morality of food" prized wild-harvested (local) above cultivated foods. As Greek philosophers pondered the best way to live, they also paid attention to folklore and accumulated wisdom about the medicinal properties of the plants around them. Aristotle is said to have conducted the first botanical research.

Alexander the Great's conquest of Persia and other Eastern lands yielded new sources of spices for the West. We can also credit him with bringing an early version of fusion cuisine westward, as Persian ingredients, customs, and techniques traveled back to Greece and the Mediterranean when his soldiers returned home.

By the second century BC, the Romans had taken a leading role in trade, including the spice trade—underscoring their power, while also helping to maintain it. Romans, as well as those in other parts of the empire, enjoyed the benefits of trade. In fact, some have said that the annals of the Roman

Empire could also be called the annals of gluttony. The demand for exotic cultivated foods soared. Pliny the Elder railed against the market for luxury food that encouraged cultivation of such large specimens of vegetables like asparagus that a poor man could not afford them.

Spices helped make possible the art of culinary disguise, which became quite popular in ancient Rome. The Latin poet Martial, remembered for his epigrams, had a cook who could make a simple gourd into any kind of dish. He succeeded so well that people were convinced they were eating beans and lentils, mushrooms, tuna, or even sweet cakes, rather than the meat of a gourd.

As they secured the Empire, the Roman legions also spread Roman food customs. The Romans had access to white and black pepper, as well as Melegueta pepper (often known as "grains of paradise") and long peppers (cubebs) from Africa, introducing to far-flung peoples a love of that irresistible tingle of a pepper on the tongue.

As the Roman Empire collapsed, many of its sophisticated trade networks began to break apart. But the hunger for spices persisted, and since these crops could not be cultivated locally, the spice trade never completely disappeared. In 735, as the Venerable Bede lay dying in Anglo-Saxon England, he directed that his personal valuables, including incense and some grains of pepper, be distributed to his fellow monks.

During the Middle Ages, spices were still a sought-after commodity. Although they were too expensive for widespread use, they were in demand for flavoring wine and beer. Scholars do not think that spices were used to compensate for the taste of less-than-fresh or heavily salted meat, as some have proposed. In fact, the use of spices in this period was relatively sophisticated. There seemed to be a rather complex theory governing the use of spices in the Middle Ages, a theory that encouraged their judicious use and relegated certain spices to particular seasons of the year.

As Europe moved into the Renaissance, spices fueled the growth of trading fortunes. It helped that sixteenth-century pharmacists thought nutmeg could cure the plague. They may or may not have been right about that, but twenty-first-century research is showing that spices like nutmeg have a beneficial effect on blood pressure, digestion, and joint and muscle pain.

Whether the clamor for spices derived from their exotic flavors or from the health benefits attributed to them, the business of transporting and selling these exotic goods continued to flourish. Wealth from the spice trade helped build some of the great cities of Europe—first Venice, then Lisbon and Amsterdam—as the search for spices prompted European explorers to turn their gaze from East to West. The riches of the New World included new taste sensations like allspice and chile peppers and, yes, chocolate. But after the flush of discovery had subsided, European cuisines became less outward looking and more codified and regionalized.

Upper-class French cuisine turned toward a narrower range of ingredients. Haute cuisine abandoned the broad palette of spices that had trickled into Western Europe and relied instead on butter, cream, and the sauces that could be made from them, as well as a limited number of herbs like tarragon, thyme, and marjoram. It was a form of eating locally that would dominate the notion of fine food through most of the twentieth century.

Recently, some Parisian chefs have made news by attempting another transformation of French food—not with radically new techniques but by adding the global ingredients long missing from haute cuisine. These twenty-first-century chefs are rediscovering how the simple addition of a spice like cardamom or cumin can utterly change a dish, bringing the global element back to the neighborhood.

It's fitting that it was an apostle of fine French cooking, Julia Child, who demystified the masterful techniques of haute cuisine and helped twentieth-century Americans broaden their culinary horizons—and eventually embrace the taste revolutions that now enliven the food scenes in American cities. The revolution in American taste has also prompted American cooks to rediscover the importance of top-quality ingredients, including good, flavorful spices and herbs. The United States is now a melting pot of culture and cuisine, as the flavors of Asia, India, Latin America, and Africa mingle with the established, yet interwoven traditions of Anglo-Saxon, Germanic, Scandinavian, and Eastern European foods.

Like many Americans, we have lived our own versions of this transformation.

Both of us grew up in the South, surrounded by people who cooked good food day after day. Much of the year they had access to fresh, local vegetables, and often to chicken, pork, and beef raised nearby. These confident cooks seemed to have no trouble turning it all into a table groaning with good things to eat.

Sara's earliest memories of chicken are the free-range hens from her grandmother's backyard in L.A. (Lower Alabama). Another grandmother presided over patio pea-shelling sessions on summer mornings, with produce freshly picked from the extended-family garden. By noontime, those same peas would be steaming on the midday "dinner" table.

A fifth-generation Texan, Katie learned early the value of a super-hot skillet for making crusty cornbread, or for frying the crispiest chicken. She rolled out pie dough with her mother and baked chocolate cakes with her grandmother.

Many of our fondest childhood memories come from the kitchen, hanging out with mothers, aunts, grandmothers, and even dads and uncles, soaking up stories, hoping for a chance to stir something or lick an empty batter bowl. We also loved the family meals that followed, the sense that food is something to share with people you love, and that meals are a time not just for eating but also for talking, catching up, and taking pleasure in the moment. But if we had a time machine and the chance now to revisit those convivial kitchens, we would love to take along some of the marvelous herbs and spices that weren't present in our mothers' cabinets— or at least weren't used on a regular basis.

Katie would surely throw a teaspoon or two of coriander into the black-eyed peas and the cornbread too—and maybe some fennel seeds for good measure. When her Grandmother Coco baked her famous chocolate "sheath cake," Katie would be tugging on her apron, urging her to stir in some chile pepper and cinnamon for an adventurous taste of "sweet heat."

Sara can't help but wonder how her mother's school-night casseroles would taste with a teaspoon or two of tarragon, or maybe some chile pepper and cumin. What fun she would have suggesting unexpected spices for Aunt Nadine to stir into her perfectly plain pound cakes and banana breads—or those ubiquitous Christmas fruitcakes.

We would both be sprinkling chile pepper on slices of watermelon, adding cumin or thyme to the butter we slathered on corn on the cob—and experimenting with new flavors on all the other foods we loved but that everyone seemed to think had to taste the same every time.

Having plunged into the spice business together, we love nothing more in our own kitchens than taking the foods of our childhoods—especially the stained recipes with notes like "Try this; your dad really liked it"—and reinventing them for our families and friends by reimagining the range of spices and herbs we can add. For the most part, our experiments have been a success, making mealtimes more interesting—and turning the task of cooking them from a chore into an adventure.

fun fact

In the first century BC, the royal physician of King Mithradates of Pontus (now in modern Turkey) formulated an antidote for every poison. The Mithridaticum, as it was called, included anise; cardamom, cassia, frankincense, saffron, ginger, and cinnamon, and Mithradates took some every day to guard against treachery. But it backfired when, unable to bear the shame after losing a disastrous battle, he decided to poison himself and couldn't.

We hope these recipes will encourage you to do the same. Think of them as starting places for your own experiments with spices and herbs. If a recipe calls for cinnamon and cumin, feel free to use another combination—maybe anise seed and coriander, or perhaps allspice and ginger. It won't always be perfect. But meals—and the time spent preparing them—will be a lot more fun. Even if you occasionally strike out, you'll also have some spectacular home runs.

That last bit of advice comes from experience. Sara's son still complains about the day his morning oatmeal had an overdose of cardamom. (Sara insists there is no such thing as too much cardamom.) Katie's kids have been overheard whispering to their friends to be careful when eating dinner with them—some things can "taste weird." Somehow, though, our children's friends are always eager to stay for dinner and the food disappears.

Our company, The Seasoned Palate, Inc., specializes in packaging dried organic spices, herbs, and zests in premeasured, one-teaspoon packets, and so you will notice that most every recipe in this book calls for exactly one teaspoon of a dried spice, herb, or zest. We package our products that way partly for the cook's convenience, but mostly because it protects them from light, air, and humidity, the elements that combine to turn a fresh-tasting spice, herb, or zest into a stale shadow of itself. Fresh spices make food better, and we have discovered that in traditional recipes calling for only a partial teaspoon, a full teaspoon almost always improves the taste. As for those recipes that call for $\frac{1}{8}$ of a teaspoon of something—unless it's referring to cayenne or some other very hot pepper, why bother?

Spices are good, and good for you. Embrace them! Increasingly, we're seeing references to nutritional research showing the benefits of spices. If you're watching your weight, researchers have produced evidence that spices help you feel satisfied with less food. Apart from controlled studies, we know from experience that when you use more spices, you can easily cut down on sugar and fat.

Consider Enlightened Oatmeal (page 35), our fancy name for a simple, nourishing, and delicious breakfast. Until we started cooking with spices in earnest, we tended to avoid oatmeal because we always ended up compensating for the plain taste by pouring on lots of sugar and cream. Spices solved that problem so well that now we almost never add sugar, and we find that low-fat milk is fine. Even better, we look forward to breakfast—and all that good fiber keeps us happy till lunchtime. Similarly, we think you'll find that you won't need as much syrup on our Gingerbread Waffles (page 40) and Spiced Pancakes (page 41) as you would use on regular waffles or pancakes.

Good health and great flavor are solid reasons to become better acquainted with spices and herbs and to use more of them in your food. But there's another reason, too: spices connect us to the past, to our ancestors and their ancestors. The spices in our food reflect the primal human itch to explore and experiment. When you add a spice or herb to your food, you're participating in one of history's oldest culinary traditions.

Far from being an exotic extra, spices from around the world make it easier—and much more fun—to turn out delicious and healthy food. They also connect us to the wider world, making it possible to explore customs and cultures around the globe without leaving your own kitchen. On page 119, you'll find an easy recipe for curry powder, a spice blend that can take any number of forms. Rather than buying a premixed curry, we hope you'll try blending your own, and thereby learn how tweaking the amount of a single spice can affect the flavor of a finished dish. We encourage you to try our curry recipe, but then to adapt it to your own taste. You'll have a deeper understanding of the flavors that are fundamental to Indian cooking. The same goes for the chili powder recipe on page 95. Try ours—we think you'll love it. Then play with it and make it your own. When you're comfortable with spices, you can easily change an ordinary weeknight meal to a Caribbean-themed jerk chicken (page 115) or an Indian tandoori dish (page 116). Use locally raised, free-range chicken and you'll experience the best taste of all—local food and global flavor.

When you see how spices can dress up your old favorites, you'll understand what we mean when we talk about "spice enlightenment"—simple but flavorful additions to familiar foods that will make you think you're tasting them for the very first time.

dried vs. fresh

What's better, dried or fresh? For most foods, there's an easy answer—fresh! Most of us don't have the choice of using fresh spices—it's dried or nothing. But for herbs, the answer isn't quite as easy. We're big fans of homegrown herbs. Sara's patio is a staging area for a summer basil crop, and any day now her potted rosemary bush will make its seasonal move outdoors.

But we've learned something about dried herbs. Most herbs that are dried commercially are grown in warmer climates closer to the equator and, in many cases, nearer to their native habitat. Whether it's the extra hours of sunlight, the higher temperatures, or just being closer to the soil in which they first sprang up, the herbs we've tasted from sunnier climes usually have more intense and complex flavors than those grown in more temperate areas.

That doesn't mean dried herbs can always replace our local bounty. After all, there's nothing better than a fresh-picked basil leaf on a slice of ripe tomato, or a batch of homemade pesto from homegrown basil. But if you like the flavor of an herb, we've learned a handy trick. The flavors of a top-quality, organic dried herb can complement the fresh herb in surprisingly delicious ways, adding layers of flavor and complexity to any dish.

The recipes in this book are designed for dried herbs, but we encourage you to experiment with both fresh and dried varieties. In fact, feel free to substitute fresh herbs for dry. Typically, you should use a three-to-one ratio of fresh to dried, or 1 tablespoon of fresh herbs for each teaspoon of dried.

Better yet, use a mixture of dried and fresh. Keep in mind that the dried herbs will usually have more flavor, but let your palate be your guide. In short, don't let the fresh-or-dry debate derail your approach to well-flavored food. Fresh or dry, herbs are magical tools that can turn any cook into a flavor artist.

Spice Basics

Allspice and cardamom

The Cast of Characters

In most cookbooks, authors take pains to introduce methods, or materials, or equipment, or philosophy. In this one, we must introduce the stars of the show, a colorful cast of flavors that can take you around the world—and you won't even have to leave your own kitchen.

This "cast of characters" is a handy guide to the herbs and spices you'll find in these recipes. Our intent in this book is to encourage you to get to know all of these flavors, what they can do for food on their own, and how you can combine them with other seasonings to create new combinations—and new possibilities for pleasing your palate.

We like to think of our palates, and all those taste buds, as a blank canvas. With each meal, we are painting on that canvas with flavors, textures, and even colors. Seasonings—herbs, spices, zests— expand the range of possibilities. Artists don't like to paint pictures with only a couple of colors. They want a rich, full palette of hues from which to choose.

That's how we want you to think of spices—as a wonderful way of broadening your culinary palette. Whether your intention is to paint culinary masterpieces, to enhance some old favorite recipes, or just to try a few kitchen adventures for the fun of it, you will appreciate how delicious, fresh-tasting spices can improve your food. And if you take time to learn the personality of each herb or spice, you'll soon have an instinctive feel for how and when you like it best. The more you know about a spice, the easier it is to incorporate it into your repertoire of recipes.

We hear a lot these days about the global kitchen and the once-foreign flavors that can add great satisfaction to our meals. We also hear a lot about the virtues of eating locally grown foods—and we heartily embrace the eat-local principle. We think spices can play well with both of those themes. Not many cooks have ready access to a local cinnamon crop, but people have been transporting spices around the world for thousands of years—a much more efficient process than shipping heavy, perishable produce and meat. In short, the spice trade makes it possible to transform local foods into global cuisine.

There's also a case for global trading in herbs, despite the fact that, like many cooks, we both grow and use fresh herbs. The fact is, when we compare the basil or sage from our Mid-Atlantic backyards to varieties grown closer to the Equator, we have to admit that more sun produces stronger and more complex flavors. We still use our homegrown herbs, but we bolster them with dried herbs, resulting in another layer of flavor and richer-tasting food.

There were good reasons those ancient explorers set out in creaky ships for parts unknown. Embrace the spices that first fanned the fires of global trade, and you'll find many answers to the explorer's itch.

Alluring Allspice

Fragrant and mysterious, allspice has a complex flavor all its own, but takes its name from its pepper, cinnamon, nutmeg, and clove notes. Allspice comes from *Pimenta dioica*, a tropical evergreen with dark glossy leaves and small white flowers; its berries are painstakingly hand-picked and air-dried to a rich red-brown.

Versatile allspice perfumes fruit dishes, jams, and apple and pumpkin pies. It lends subtle warmth to cakes and breads, but it's also a must in pickling spice and corned beef. Allspice creates depth and aroma in rubs and marinades for pork, beef, and venison. With cinnamon, tomatoes, and white wine, it adds exquisite flavor to lamb moussaka. And surely allspice is responsible for the popularity of that guilty pleasure, ketchup!

Most allspice comes from Jamaica, where the same rich earth that makes its coffee so renowned produces the finest allspice. Early Spanish explorers mistook the tiny berries for black pepper; the name stuck, and allspice is still sometimes called Jamaican pepper. Later, pirates used allspice to season meat they cooked on their boucans, or barbecues, earning them the name buccaneers. When the English seized Jamaica from Spain in 1655, they gained control of the only source of allspice for the next 300 years.

Today, Scandinavians import the most allspice (for pickled herring and baking), but allspice has retained its place in the English kitchen, too, in spiced beef and traditional holiday fare like Christmas pudding and mincemeat. Allspice remains a staple of Jamaican cooking, combining with other tropical tastes in the famous jerk seasoning for chicken, pork, or goat.

Try substituting allspice in recipes that call for ground cloves, cinnamon, or nutmeg.

Amazing Anise Seed

Not to be confused with the stronger star anise of Chinese cooking, anise seed, *Pimpinella anisum*, originated in western Anatolia. Its sweet, delicate flavor, reminiscent of licorice, tantalizes in baked goods like biscotti and pastries. But it is treasured, too, for the subtle sweetness it lends to pork, duck, or fish. Anise seed distinguishes the French apéritif Pernod and the liqueurs anisette and ouzo.

In ancient times, the Assyrians and Greeks valued anise seed as a medicine and an aphrodisiac. Pythagoras (yes, that Pythagoras) praised it as an antidote for scorpion stings. But it was the Romans who really got creative with anise, using it to settle the stomach, freshen the breath, quell coughs, and repel moths. Tributaries could even pay taxes with it.

Fortunately, the Romans also developed the culinary uses of this lively seed, spicing wine and baking it into after-dinner cakes that may be the ancestors of the modern wedding cake. Medieval Europeans associated anise seed with youth and vigor; it toned the skin and revived travelers on the grueling journeys of the day. Sixteenth-century people continued the tradition of eclectic use with anise-baited mousetraps.

The opening of Portuguese, Dutch, and English direct trade with Asia led to the increasing popularity of anise seed in Europe and beyond. In colonial Virginia, each man was required by law to plant at least six anise seeds; while in Spanish America, anise added a sweet new note to an old Aztec drink, chocolate. Today, anise seed enlivens Greek, Scandinavian, Arabic, and East Indian cuisines. It goes well with eggs, chicken, fish, and pork and adds unexpected zip to carrots and spinach—and even our favorite mac and cheese. It makes pies, pastries, cookies, and sponge cake irresistible.

Try adding 1 teaspoon each of anise seed, cinnamon, and orange zest and ½ teaspoon ground cloves to your favorite sweet bread recipe for a teatime treat.

Extravagant Basil

Basil's vibrant taste and ravishing scent, with subtle undertones of anise and cloves, call to mind the perfumed warmth of a summer garden. We know it as the quintessential herb for the warm-weather bounty of zucchini, fat eggplants, glossy peppers, and best of all, tomatoes. Sprinkle it over ripe wedges drizzled with balsamic vinegar and fruity olive oil. Or slow cook it in a lazy Sunday sauce to serve with spaghetti al dente, crusty bread, and a good Chianti or Barolo. Either way, basil and tomatoes are a royal pairing. In winter, serve pasta tossed with basil, sun-dried tomatoes, porcini mushrooms, and tangy Romano cheese as you dream of la dolce vita.

The plant *Ocimum basilicum*, a native of Persia and India, gets its name from the Greek basileus, "kingly," and it was said to be reserved for kings alone to harvest with golden sickles. The Romans knew basil at least as early as the first century AD, and in medieval times the fragrant leaves were used as a strewing herb. As with its relative, mint, basil has many varieties. The three kinds of Thai basil have more pronounced clove or lemon notes than the "sweet" basil that is common around the Mediterranean.

Use basil to evoke the sensual joy of the Italian or Provençal table. Its heady flavor bursts from

chicken stewed with tomatoes and olives, or from pistou, a seasoning of basil, garlic, and olive oil, ground in a mortar and stirred into vegetable soup or minestrone just before serving. Basil suits egg, cheese, or pasta dishes, especially those with opulent ricotta or creamy fresh mozzarella.

Accent vinaigrette dressing with basil and a touch of mint and orange zest; or try quirky but addictively refreshing fresh pineapple slices sprinkled with basil and drizzled with sweet balsamic vinegar.

Queen Cardamom

Sweetly seductive with a slightly pungent scent reminiscent of pine needles, green cardamom is hailed as the Queen of Spices. From the Cardamom Hills of India's Western Ghat mountains, cardamom's domain ranges from Indian feasts with their fragrant platters to snug Scandinavian kitchens to the narrow lanes of Middle Eastern bazaars where buyers and sellers seek respite from the heat over a cup of cardamom-spiced coffee.

With the versatility to enliven sweet or savory dishes, cardamom is one of the world's most widely used spices. Cardamom adds its ambrosial warmth to baked goods, rice, meat, fish, and vegetable dishes. In Scandinavia, bakers prefer it to cinnamon for their breads and cakes.

Elettaria cardamomum grows in perennial stands of reedy shoots with long, dark green leaves. The spice comes from its pods, which must be snipped off by hand, then air-cured. All this care makes cardamom the third most costly spice on earth, after saffron and vanilla, as well as one of the most beloved. Sanskrit religious texts mentioned cardamom in the fourth century BC. About a thousand years ago an Indian compendium noted its medicinal uses, and recipes began appearing not long afterward. Around this time Arab traders encountered the spice and enthusiastically spread it throughout Southeast Asia and to the ancient Persians and Greeks. The Romans distinguished between two kinds of cardamom, using green cardamom to spice wine and sauce meatballs and black cardamom to perfume men's hair.

In India, by 1500, the Sultan of Mandu was enjoying cardamom in rice and sherbets; soon after, the Portuguese in Asia began to take note. By the mid-sixteenth century cardamom was commonly traded on both maritime and overland intercontinental spice routes. Amazingly, all cardamom was harvested from wild plants controlled by the Raja of Kerala until about 200 years ago, when the British began cultivating it in other regions of India that had come under their rule. Today, India and Guatemala are the two main producers of cardamom.

Although both green and black cardamom (*amomum*) are members of the ginger family, black cardamom is a different species with a smoky, coarser flavor and cannot be substituted for green or "true" cardamom.

Cardamom perfectly complements yogurt's tanginess. Try it in a yogurt-ginger-lime–based marinade, or in a carrot-apple slaw flavored with lemon and dressed with yogurt and mayonnaise. Add a little salt, honey, and a handful of raisins, if you like. For an appealing fruit dip, stir some cardamom into yogurt sweetened with honey.

You can use cardamom in place of all or part of the cloves or cinnamon called for in recipes.

To substitute ground for whole green cardamom, use 1 teaspoon of ground for every 6 or 7 pods of the whole spice.

Feisty Chile Peppers

More nice than naughty, mild chile peppers will gently tingle your tongue and add depth to foods that need a bit of warmth to truly blossom. Fruitier and more flavorful than cayenne pepper, milder chile peppers are perfect for brightening creamy sauces like béchamel or mayonnaise and salad dressing. A pinch of mild chile pepper takes macaroni and cheese, canned soups, casseroles, and meat loaf from blah and bland to sassy. Use it to pick up the pace of morning scrambled eggs, or substitute it for cayenne to make brazen deviled dishes mild and impish.

Mild chile peppers belong to the species *Capsicum annuum,* whose hundreds of varieties range from gentle bell peppers to five-alarm habaneros. Botanically, the chile pepper is a berry, and belongs to *Solanaceae,* the same family as potatoes and tomatoes. Like its cousins, it is rich in vitamins A and C.

Chile peppers' hotness is measured in Scoville Heat Units (SHU), named after the pharmacist Wilbur Scoville, who invented the system in 1912. Sweet bell peppers score 0, jalapeño peppers around 3,000–6,000, and a habanero pepper a flame-throwing 500,000. Milder chile peppers, including ancho, typically register around 15,000 SHU or below.

Although they have been cultivated for more than 5,000 years, chile peppers were unknown outside of the Americas before 1492. Spanish and Portuguese traders introduced them to Europe and Asia. Today, one-fifth of the world's people eat chile peppers. They are used in Indian, Thai, Chinese, Italian, and Hungarian cuisines and lend festive notes to southwestern, Mexican, Caribbean, and South American foods.

Chile and cinnamon

Outside the kitchen, Indian families hang chile peppers and a lemon over the threshold of their homes to keep harm away. Italian-Americans sometimes wear gold charms shaped like chile peppers to ward off the evil eye. Chile pepper is reputed to relieve arthritis, revive a flagging love life, and cure intestinal worms. Scientists note that preliminary studies indicate chile pepper may help regulate the body's production of insulin.

Eating chile pepper releases endorphins in the brain, producing a feeling of pleasant well-being. But forget drinking water to quell chile pepper's heat: its fiery active ingredient, capsaicin, isn't water-soluble. Instead, follow the lead of Indian, Thai, and Mexican cooks and serve cooling dairy-based side dishes like yogurt raita, or cucumbers in yogurt; creamy Thai iced tea; or rich cheese or sour cream on the side. Or eat plain rice, bread, or sweets to tame the flame.

Outstanding Ancho

Ancho, one of our favorite of the relatively mild chile peppers, is prized in Mexico and the Southwest for its sweet, sexy smolder, hinting of fruit and smoke. More complex and much milder than cayenne, it adds smoky zest to rubs and marinades for beef, pork, chicken, and turkey, and sparks up robust greens like spinach, collards, or chard. In pre-Columbian times, chile peppers added flavor and vitamins to the sacred triad of corn, beans, and squash that were the daily fare of the Maya and Aztecs.

Ancho chile is superb at bringing out food's underlying flavors. Use it to jazz up cornbread batters, stews, or your favorite chili powder blend, or combine it with true cinnamon for a "sweet heat" effect. Team ancho chile pepper with lime juice in marinades for fish or flank steak, or in melted butter for zesty corn on the cob.

Charming Cassia Cinnamon

If the aroma of fresh-baked cassia cinnamon buns transports you to another world, it should be no surprise—the ancient Greeks believed the wind blowing from paradise was cassia scented. The most popular type of cinnamon in the U.S., cassia is heavenly for baking, but it's also divine in marinades and meat dishes. The best cassia cinnamon has an aromatic, sweet note that is slightly more assertive, with a bit more bite than "true" cinnamon.

Cassia cinnamon is the tender inner bark of *Cinnamomum cassia,* a tree of the laurel family originally native to China. Around the Mediterranean, Romans burned it as incense; the Egyptians included it in burial unguents, and the ancient Hebrews anointed sacred places with cinnamon-scented oil. Traditional Chinese medicine uses it to reinforce yang, treat kidney ailments, improve circulation, and stimulate the fire element in the body. In medieval times, knights and ladies spiced meat with camelyne, a sauce made from cinnamon, garlic, ginger, vinegar, and breadcrumbs that was all the rage at castle banquets.

Cassia cinnamon warms the taste of apples and summer fruits like blueberries or peaches, but it also has an affinity for oranges, onions, carrots, spinach, and squash. Choose cassia cinnamon for recipes with robust flavors—like a Corsican beef stew with earthy dried mushrooms, bacon, white wine, tomatoes, and rosemary, ladled over pasta with grated Parmesan. Or follow an Asian lead: combine cinnamon with ginger, soy sauce, and garlic to make a succulent marinade for pork or chicken. Cassia cinnamon adds subtle interest to curries, pilafs, couscous, and split pea or lentil dishes. Stir cassia and brown sugar into hot dark-roast coffee for a Mexican after-dinner treat. But don't stop in the kitchen—sprinkle cassia cinnamon on rose petals spread out to dry for an angelic potpourri.

Classic "True" Cinnamon

Neil Young sang about being happy with a cinnamon girl, and once you catch the intoxicating perfume of true cinnamon you'll know why. Woody, warm, and lively, true cinnamon is sweeter, more delicate, and lighter in color than cassia cinnamon. Matchless in baked goods and desserts, true cinnamon is the most prevalent variety in Europe; elsewhere it inspires Mexican, Asian, Turkish, and Moroccan cuisines.

True cinnamon, *Cinnamomum zeylanicum* or *C. verum,* is the bark of a tree originating in the moist air and sandy soil of Sri Lanka; the name "cinnamon" comes from a Malay word that means "sweet wood." Since ancient times, outrigger canoes carried cinnamon from Ceylon, as it was known, through Indonesia to East Africa, where Arab traders shipped it by caravan through the Nile Valley to Egypt, or via the Red Sea to Somalia and on to the Mediterranean. In the Middle Ages, Venice grew wealthy on this trade. After 1500, the Portuguese captured Ceylon, breaking the Venetian monopoly, but were in turn driven out by the Dutch in 1636. By the end of the eighteenth century, the island changed hands again, falling under control of the English East India Company, which used its network of botanical gardens to spread the lucrative cinnamon trees to other places.

Today, true cinnamon is sometimes known as Sri Lankan cinnamon, Ceylon cinnamon, or Saigon cinnamon, depending on where it was grown. All these names distinguish it from cassia, a cousin of the cinnamon tree, which in the United States has become commonly known as cinnamon. If, like most Americans, you have grown up on cassia cinnamon, introduce yourself to true cinnamon and you'll likely have a new favorite spice friend.

Substitute ripe pears for half the apples in your favorite apple pie recipe, and spice the pie with delicate true cinnamon for a luscious home-baked treat. Cinnamon also has a natural affinity for lamb, sprinkled on chops or roasts, or in piquant Turkish lamb stew with tomato, apricots, and pistachios. A pinch or two in tomato sauce or on baked acorn squash brings out the natural sweetness in both. Hot buttered toast soars to new heights with true cinnamon and sugar; or try cinnamon blended with honey and butter as a tasty spread.

Clever Cloves

Part of cloves' appeal is their scent. In braised meat, stews, and vegetables, in sweet desserts and baked goods, cloves lure with their spicy promise. The darkly romantic, headstrong taste of cloves hints at the mystery and drama that have surrounded this precious spice since ancient times.

Once a scarce luxury, cloves today appear in fine Asian, European, and American cooking. The Spanish braise lamb in red Rioja wine, onion, garlic, and cloves, and serve it alongside saffron rice and crisp green beans. French charcuterie relies on cloves in the *quatre épices,* or four-spice powder, for seasoning fine sausages and piquant marinades.

Cloves are dried from the rose-colored flower buds of *Syzygium aromaticum.* These evergreens, native to the volcanic slopes of the Moluccas, are so pungent that sailors could smell them far out at sea. Although cloves have been traded widely for nearly 4,000 years, for most of that time no one knew for sure where they came from. Even after Arabic and European traders learned of the source, the Moluccas—and the spice they produced—retained their exotic aura, perpetuated by authors like Milton and Cervantes.

Cloves' profitability drew less benign attention: the Spanish, Portuguese, and Dutch each controlled the Moluccas in turn. In 1770, a daring French former missionary, aided by natives bitterly resentful of Dutch rule, smuggled out hundreds of clove seedlings, which were planted in Mauritius, and later Madagascar and the Seychelles. After the Napoleonic wars, the British eventually brought clove trees to Grenada in the Caribbean. All these places supply cloves to today's brisk world market.

Cloves are versatile. They build complexity in rich bourguignonne sauce, simmered from red wine, bacon, onions, and mushrooms. A hint of cloves lends an air of intrigue in beets, winter squash, ham dishes, rice, soups, and cranberry sauce or fruit compotes. We like the way this clever spice can wake up a chocolate cake or a batch of chocolate chip cookies.

Cheerful Coriander

Warm, citrus-noted coriander's sweetly spicy flavor makes it a natural for sweet desserts and savory meat, fish, and vegetable dishes. The plant, *Coriandrum sativum,* is used as both an herb and a spice, but its green leaves, known as cilantro, have a completely different taste from the spice ground from its "seed," which is actually a tiny fruit.

One of the oldest known spices, coriander originated in the eastern Mediterranean and spread by trade and conquest throughout the ancient world. The Greeks burned it as incense to please the gods, and Egyptians placed it in the tomb of Tutankhamen for use in the afterlife. In the book of Exodus, the manna that sustained the ancient Israelites on their trek through the desert was compared to coriander seeds; today it is commemorated as one of the traditional herbs of the Passover seder. Coriander reached

India by way of Persia in the fourth century BC. Later, during China's Han dynasty, it was believed coriander could confer immortality, but only if consumed by the virtuous. In the West, Roman legions carried coriander throughout Europe, from whence it crossed the Atlantic: by 1670 settlers were growing coriander in colonial Massachusetts.

Today, coriander is synonymous with Indian cooking and curries. Beloved in Middle Eastern and Moroccan dishes, it also flavors the marinades and rich pork dishes of France's Burgundy region. Elsewhere in Europe and America it appears in stews and sausages, often paired with thyme. It is an ingredient of pickling spice, and its sweet fragrance wafts from ovens where apple pies and gingerbread bake.

Try coriander in marinated mushrooms or tomato salad. Or for a new twist on a summer favorite, combine allspice, coriander, dill, and basil with baked or sautéed eggplant.

Add a teaspoon of ground coriander to the batter for banana, carrot, or zucchini bread.

Place salmon fillets in foil or parchment packets with sliced fresh tomatoes, fresh mint leaves, coriander, and black pepper. Bake, and open the savory, steaming packets at the table. Or marinate firm-fleshed fish in coriander, allspice, lemon juice, and extra-virgin olive oil.

Comforting Cumin

Warm and flavorful, with subtle notes of cedar and anise, the nuance of cumin lingers like perfume. This golden spice originated in the Nile Valley but has become indispensable the world over: in Mexican mole, Texas chili powder, Indian

Anise seed and fennel

Dill weed

garam masala and curry, and Moroccan *ras el hanout*, a complex spice mixture custom-blended in bazaars and used in rice and couscous, lamb, game, and almond-and-honey sweets.

Cumin is ground from the seeds of the flowering annual *Cuminum cyminum*, a relative of parsley sometimes grouped with dill, caraway, fennel, and anise. Cumin was known in biblical times and spread along spice routes to the ancient Mediterranean, Asia Minor, South Asia, and beyond. More recently, cumin has enriched the baking of Central and Eastern Europe; it may have arrived there in the second century during the campaigns of Roman emperor Marcus Aurelius.

Cumin's affinity for dried beans shines in split pea soup and in dal, a richly spiced purée of yellow lentils. It flavors many snacks, vegetable dishes, yogurt condiments, and cooling drinks of Pakistan and northern India. In Greece, sausages of minced lamb, onion, and garlic are spiced with fragrant cumin and served in savory tomato sauce, while in Spain, cumin, saffron, and cinnamon season rich stews.

Use cumin in a marinade of lemon juice and soy sauce for grilled beef, or add it to a spice rub. It is traditional in ham or chicken croquettes and lends savor to meat loaf. Cumin delights in cabbage, carrots, cauliflower, buttered corn, and cheese spreads.

Cumin gives egg salad and deviled eggs enticing flavor and color—fleck with chives for a festive contrast. Or in place of stodgy potato salad, try a lively Indian version: a pound or so of potatoes, boiled, cooled, and cubed, tossed in a bowl with lemon juice, 2 teaspoons ground cumin, ½ teaspoon chile pepper, 2 tablespoons chopped cilantro, and salt and pepper to taste.

Graceful Dill Weed

Feathery, spruce-colored dill weed has a fresh, green taste with a subtle note of anise. This herb grows well in cool areas, making it a staple of northern and eastern European cooking in dishes such as borscht and savory breads. Dill weed is delicious in sour cream- or mustard-based sauces for fish, and it's essential in gravlax, the celebrated cured salmon dish of Scandinavia.

The leaves of *Anethum graveolens* are known as "dill weed" to distinguish them from dill seeds, which have a distinct, stronger flavor. Dill weed's winsome freshness complements foods that might be overwhelmed by a less tactful herb: eggs, mild cheeses, delicate fish (sauced in white wine or cream), baby carrots, or tiny new potatoes, boiled and tossed in dill, butter, salt, and pepper. Dill can transform egg, tuna, or potato salads from sturdy staples into elegant diversions.

Romans thought dill brought luck, and they adorned themselves with its graceful fronds. The word "dill" may derive from an old Scandinavian word meaning "to trill or lull"; it was used to treat insomnia, and in England, infants were given dill water to help them sleep. Dill is still used today to calm hiccups, ease stomachaches, and treat gas.

In 1640 an English writer noted that dill ". . . is put among pickled Cowcumbers, wherewith it doth very well agree, giving unto the cold fruit a pretty, spicie taste or rellish." We agree, and add that cucumbers are also delicious in classic dill vinaigrette and creamy dill dressings, as in Greek tzatziki, a cooling yogurt-cucumber side dish.

Fragrant Fennel

Fennel seed's vibrant, aromatic anise note enlivens both sweet and savory dishes, especially in Italian,

Indian, Middle Eastern, and northern European cooking. It is delicious in cabbage, vegetable, or lentil dishes, tasty with potatoes or rice, and fragrant in breads and sweet pastries.

Fennel seed lends itself to rich-tasting fish, like salmon, tuna, mackerel, or lake trout. Italians use it to flavor savory pork sausages, rabbit, and venison, and they crumble cooked bacon and fennel seeds over dough to make pizza Genovese, a focaccia served as an accompaniment to soups or stews.

Fennel seed originated in the Mediterranean. Actually, it's not a seed at all, but the tiny fruit of the fennel plant, *Foeniculum vulgare,* whose green, bulb-shaped stalk and feathery leaves are also delicious. Although fennel seed is sweet, Indian cooks consider it one of the "hot" spices (along with cardamom, cloves, and others) because it is thought to provide heat to the body. Fennel seed is also one of the "five spices" in the Chinese seasoning of that name.

Medicinal and other uses for fennel seed abound. In Shakespearean times it aided digestion and increased the milk of nursing mothers, who drank a tea of fennel seeds in barley water. And not only is it a breath freshener, it's said to repel pesky bugs—and witches!

For fragrant fish, combine a bay leaf, a pinch of mustard seed or powdered mustard, lemon zest, white wine, and fennel seed, and pour over fish; seal in parchment or foil packets, bake, and tear open to enjoy the sweet-sharp savor.

Fennel seed gives a fresh new take on a classic dessert—try adding a little to apple pie; or savor the aroma of a dark, Swedish rye bread with fennel seed and orange zest.

Heavenly Ginger

Ginger is the ambassador of the spice world. It figures in dozens of cuisines from Indian to Chinese, German to Jamaican, and even beyond: according to Arabic texts, beautiful maidens serve ginger-infused wine to the virtuous in Paradise. This versatile spice with its fresh, piquant flavor is ground from the "root" (actually a rhizome) of *Zingiber officinale,* a plant native to Southeast Asia, known for its gorgeous, lily-like flowers.

Ginger's unique flavor lends itself equally well to savory or sweet foods: scenting delicate fish dishes, giving bite to savory beef stews and sassy chicken stir-fries, and adding zest to creamy desserts or even cheesecake or cobblers. Ginger has a special affinity for lemon, orange, and other citrus flavors—use it in lively marinades for fish or chicken. Added to lime juice and sweetened with honey, it adds spark to fresh bananas, ripe melon, or other seasonal fruits.

Cooks have treasured ginger's pungent, bright taste for thousands of years. Recipes using ginger appear in the Hindu epic *Mahabharata,* written around the fourth century BC. Traders grew it in boxes aboard their ships, spreading it along ancient sea routes north to China, Korea, and Japan, and south and west to the Indian Ocean and the Pacific Islands. From Asia, ginger traveled by ship and caravan to the Middle East, Africa, and eventually Europe, where it was beloved by ancient Roman cooks and pharmacists 2,000 years ago. Ginger was a staple of medieval feasts, and its warming qualities were valued in antinausea medicines and as an aphrodisiac. Today, ginger is used in India and China to relieve nausea and motion sickness; English and American moms give ginger ale as a home remedy to settle the stomach; and scientists note ginger's antioxidant and anti-inflammatory properties.

Ginger

To substitute for fresh ginger, use ½ teaspoon ground ginger to 1 teaspoon fresh or 1 to 2 teaspoons preserved ginger.

Add ginger to your favorite banana bread recipe for a new layer of flavor. Ginger also adds an enticing aroma to shortbreads, sugar cookies, or even cheesecake.

Ginger, a few tablespoons of orange juice, orange zest, and a dash of sesame oil highlight the unique flavor of stir-fried asparagus.

Ginger loves citrus! Mash a teaspoon of ground ginger with half a stick of butter and a teaspoon or two of lemon or orange zest, and melt it at the last minute as a sauce for sautéed chicken, fish, or scallops.

Joyful Marjoram

Essential to a good poultry stuffing, marjoram is also delicious rubbed on the skin and insides of your bird before roasting. It's especially nice with grilled fish, and its subtle flavor complements egg dishes and fresh vegetables like carrots, mushrooms, and squash. Marjoram excels in spinach soufflés or fritters and intrigues in tomato-based dishes and sauce. Green beans tossed in good olive oil and a teaspoon of marjoram are a perfect accompaniment for roasts or grilled meat.

It is said that marjoram was first grown on Mount Olympus by Aphrodite, the beautiful goddess of love, and its divinely seductive scent, hinting of flowers and pine, makes this hard to deny. A sweeter, milder cousin of oregano, marjoram (*Oregano majorana*) is a small, slow-growing plant with tiny oval leaves and miniature white or pink blossoms. Its delicate, mildly spicy taste evokes the sun-washed garden cooking of the Riviera.

Wherever marjoram grows, people associate it with happiness. Nicknamed "joy of the mountains," it was traditionally used to weave crowns for European brides and grooms as a symbol of wedded bliss. In India, marjoram is held to be sacred to Hindu deities Shiva and Vishnu.

Despite marjoram's delicate flavor, it blends beautifully into classic French fines herbes mixtures. Combined with thyme and basil, it adds inspiration to salad dressings and to minestrone and other bean soups.

In recipes calling for oregano, try substituting marjoram—it lends a refreshing subtlety to robust favorites.

Nuanced Nutmeg

With its warm, well-loved, sweet-spicy taste, nutmeg 'tis the seasoning for holiday treats, whether pumpkin pie, eggnog, or Christmas puddings. It's also a classic flavoring for sweet potatoes and winter squash. Fragrant on French toast, comforting in warm milk, it adds a dusting of sophistication to your frothy cappuccino.

But did you know that Italian cooks consider nutmeg essential to their savory dishes? Nutmeg is the secret ingredient in rich Alfredo sauce, plump cheese ravioli and tortellini, and dishes *alla Fiorentina*—that is, made with spinach and creamy cheese sauce. Italians like to use a touch of nutmeg on vegetables like green beans, carrots, and spinach.

Nutmeg appeared early on in France's rich Burgundy region—the thirteenth-century French chivalrous novel *Romance of the Rose* praises nutmeg as "neither bitter nor bland." Today, French cooks serve a spectacular pumpkin soup flavored with nutmeg, bay leaf, anise seed, chives, onion, and cream. Nutmeg is one of the four spices of *quatre épices,* the classic French charcuterie seasoning that also includes black pepper, ginger, and cloves. Nutmeg adds subtle savor to creamy white sauces like béchamel or Mornay, and to chicken or veal dishes.

Mysterious and costly, nutmeg began to be traded in Europe around the sixth century. Later, the English poet Chaucer mentions nutmeg-spiced ale, and in fourteenth-century Germany a pound of nutmeg was so valuable it could be exchanged for seven oxen. Still, no Europeans knew its source until the Portuguese reached the Spice Islands (Moluccas) of East Asia early in the sixteenth century. Immediately, there commenced a bloody, centuries-long struggle for control. Throughout, nutmeg retained its allure, continuing to appear in numerous recipes for foods, aphrodisiacs, and cures.

Today, most nutmeg, *Myristica fragrans,* comes from Indonesia or Grenada. The trees produce a yellow fruit; nutmeg is its hard, round seed, and the spice we call mace is the nutmeg's lacy, fibrous covering.

For an American take on this storied spice, combine nutmeg, cinnamon, and orange juice to season butternut or acorn squash, sweet potatoes, or other yellow vegetables. If you like, add a pinch of thyme—delectable!

Awesome Oregano

Oregano, sometimes known as wild marjoram, has a robust taste that gives Greek, Italian, and Mexican cuisines their characteristic verve. Excellent with grilled meats or fresh garden tomatoes, oregano is aromatic and assertive, carrying a hint of balsam. It is especially good dried, although the fillers commonly added to supermarket oregano

can obscure its talents. Not so with organic spices, especially when their flavor is protected from light, air, and humidity.

Oregano is a zesty classic in tomato-based dishes, especially pizza and pasta sauces, and soups like minestrone. Add oregano, and chicken, pork, eggs, fish, and stuffings will bloom with aroma and savor. Oregano is a traditional European sausage seasoning. It adds spunk to salads and enlivens cabbage, cauliflower, broccoli, and Brussels sprouts. With help from oregano, eggplant, zucchini, mushrooms, and even potatoes show their vivacious side.

Long ago, oregano was thought to be an antidote for poisons as well as a treatment for convulsions. In France and England, oregano perfumed soaps and sachets, and it was used to dye cloth purple or reddish brown.

Mexican oregano is actually a member of the verbena family and has a sharper flavor than *Origanum vulgare.*

On the shores of the Mediterranean, masses of oregano cover the hillsides with small purple, pink, or white flowers on vigorous spreading stems. Found originally in Mediterranean North Africa and Europe and in south and central Asia, oregano owes its memorable flavor to the essential oils that help the plant conserve water in its dry native terrain.

Rollicking Rosemary

Whatever the season, rosemary's fresh flavor invigorates. Rosemary is at its dramatic, aromatic best with grilled or pan-roasted meats—lamb, pork, and game—or crisp-skinned duck or Cornish game hens. This vivacious herb livens up meat loaf and gives just the right spark to mashed potatoes or savory baked bread and scones.

Thyme, sage, and cumin

A woody perennial, *Rosmarinus officinalis* gives off an unmistakable evergreen scent. But despite the delicacy of its slender, dark green leaves and tiny purple flowers, rosemary is no shrinking violet—its assertive taste stands up to other dynamic flavors like citrus, red wine, or balsamic vinegar to create memorable combinations.

The name "rosemary" is said to come from the Latin *Rosmarinus,* or "dew of the sea," but this is not certain. In both Arabic and Persian, its names mean "crown of the mountain," perhaps a reference to its native Mediterranean slopes. A standard in herbal gardens in ancient Rome and in medieval monasteries, rosemary's popularity as both an herb and an ornamental shows no signs of fading. Perhaps its most enduring use is as a memory enhancer: Roman students placed a sachet of rosemary beneath their pillows the night before an exam or carried sprigs into tests. Shakespeare immortalized the association in *Hamlet:* "There's rosemary, that's for remembrance; pray, love, remember," says tragic Ophelia.

Rosemary has a long tradition of medicinal uses and is said to relieve headaches and calm the nerves. English herbalist John Gerard in his *Herball or Generall Historie of Plantes* (1597) recommends rosemary to "comforte the brain." Today, Provençal families keep pots of rosemary in bedrooms for its soothing scent; and a rosemary rinse brings out the highlights in brunette hair.

Try a marinade of rosemary, olive oil, and lemon juice for tuna steaks, turkey cutlets, or chicken. Or toss grilled zucchini, peppers, or eggplant in a vinaigrette flavored with rosemary and orange zest. Try rosemary with oregano and thyme—they combine beautifully in bean dishes, stews, or casseroles.

Sprightly Sage

The ancients thought sage brought wisdom and longevity, but clever cooks reach for sage for its pleasantly pungent, lemony-pepper flavor. Sage evokes the classic American tastes of a Norman Rockwell table, its fragrance wafting from turkey stuffing, savory sausage, and steaming casseroles of beans and buttered vegetables. But versatile sage makes the English merry too, in Lincolnshire sausages and Derbyshire cheese. And Italians flip for it in veal saltimbocca and the robust northern Italian hunter's cuisine.

Sage excels as a seasoning for lamb, duck, and game. Try sage with thyme and parsley in meat loaf, or pat it onto pork chops. Add it to the breading for fried chicken, or season chicken with sage, ginger, and orange zest before baking. Sage sparkles in mushroom dishes and with vegetables like butternut squash, asparagus, or tomatoes. Creamy, sage-scented mashed potatoes make the perfect side dish for roast chicken.

An evergreen shrub with velvety silver-green leaves and lavender flowers, *Salvia officinalis* (garden or common sage) is native to the Mediterranean and the Balkans and is often grown as an ornamental plant. In Arabic it's called *shay al-jabal,* "tea from the mountain," and is brewed into a calming infusion. Cherokee people use sage as a cough and cold remedy and tonic. Sage has antibacterial and antioxidant properties and is used as an antiperspirant. Its refreshing scent enlivens perfumes, soaps, and aftershave.

For sage butter, blend a teaspoon of sage into ½ cup softened sweet butter. Spread on hot biscuits, or use it to sauté chicken livers.

In recipes calling for rosemary, substitute sage, or combine the two for an enticing herbal pairing.

Très Chic Tarragon

Tarragon—luxurious, warm, reminiscent of anise—assures elegance at your table. One of France's fines herbes, tarragon gives exquisite flavor to cream sauces for chicken, vegetables, and seafood, including the renowned lobster Thermidor. But for all its polished delicacy, tarragon invigorates too—in classic sauce béarnaise, so tangy and right over a bodacious steak or a succulent veal chop. Divine in a white wine deglaze, tarragon shines with acidic flavors: in tarragon vinegar, vinaigrette dressings, even in pineapple salsa. Stir tarragon into sour cream to spoon over baked potatoes or mushrooms; or make a zingy tarragon tartar sauce. Use lemon juice, tarragon, and shallots for poultry, or serve roast chicken with tarragon and garlic stuffing.

Tarragon is a member of the daisy and sunflower family. Originally native to Siberia, the finest tarragon is the smooth-leaved French cultivar *Artemisia dracunculus* "Sativa." Known in Moorish Spain, tarragon became popular in the rest of Europe during the Renaissance and later crossed the Atlantic. The top producers of tarragon these days are France and California.

"Tarragon is one of the perfuming or Spicy Furnitures of our Sallets," noted Jean de la Quintinie in the seventeenth century, and it's good advice. For a change from dill, try tarragon in cucumber salad, substituting shallots for onions. Tarragon mayonnaise or rémoulade spooned over lamb or poached salmon makes an elegant cold supper; or try it on ripe red tomatoes. Steep 1 teaspoon of tarragon in ¼ cup white wine, stir into 1 cup of mayonnaise, and season with salt and freshly ground pepper for a savory dip or dressing with French flair.

Despite its closeness to anise, tarragon has a unique flavor for which there is no substitute. Use tarragon judiciously—a little goes a long way.

I know a bank where the wild thyme blows,
Where oxlips and the nodding violet grows. . . .
There sleeps Titania sometime of the night,
Lull'd in these flowers with dances and delight. . . .
—Shakespeare, *A Midsummer Night's Dream*

Storied Thyme

Thyme, another of the fines herbes of French cooking, is basic to southern European cuisine and its Creole and Cajun cousins in the American South. This fresh-tasting herb, with its hint of cloves and spice, gives a robust savor to chowders and stews, yet lends refinement to the most exquisite fish, veal, or egg dishes.

Thyme's name meant "sacrifice" in ancient Greece, where it was offered as a pleasing gift to the gods. Thyme is a perennial native to arid Mediterranean hills. Many varieties exist, but *Thymus vulgaris,* common thyme, is most beloved as a culinary herb. It's hard to believe the tiny leaves and delicate pink or white flowers of this scrappy plant yield such exquisite flavor. But the harsh sun and dry soil of its natural environment seem only to strengthen the fragrant essential oil for which thyme is prized.

During the Middle Ages, people placed thyme under their pillows to ward off nightmares, but you'll use this magical herb to whip up dream dishes. Thyme is essential to the bouquet garni of fine French cooking: place a quarter-teaspoon of thyme, a sprig of parsley, and a bay leaf in cheesecloth or a tea ball, or bind between two celery sticks. Use it to infuse soups, stews, and stocks with the heady savor of sun-drenched Provence.

Thyme is naturally concentrated, so it's well suited for marinades and for long, slow cooking, gradually releasing its heavenly flavor. It's perfect in Crock-Pots. Or sauté chicken breasts, deglaze with cognac, and finish with thyme and cream. Add thyme to stuffings and sauces, or use it in classic lentil and bean dishes. A natural ally of vegetables, thyme is especially good with green beans or mushrooms sautéed in butter or olive oil.

Thyme is delicious in borscht; and it enlivens antipasto dishes like roasted peppers with minced garlic, marinated artichoke hearts, or plump, fresh olives.

For a subtle variation, try thyme in recipes that call for rosemary; or use a little of both.

In recipes calling for a tablespoon of fresh thyme leaves, substitute 1 teaspoon dried thyme.

Transcendent Turmeric

With its brilliant yellow color and woody, understated flavor, turmeric is best known as the base for Indian, Thai, and West Indian curries. It's widely used in Southeast Asian, Ethiopian, and Middle Eastern cooking, but turmeric isn't really exotic. It's common in American foods—giving vivid color to the yellow mustard on all-American hot dogs and flavoring the tasty relishes and pickles that accompany them at summer cookouts.

Turmeric (sometimes spelled "tumeric") enlivens any table, bringing its gorgeous hue and subtle zest to rice, fish, chicken, turkey, and lamb. Western cooking usually combines it with other spices such as coriander, chiles, cumin, or ginger. Turmeric is pure gold in lentil and bean dishes— try it in dal, a soup of green or yellow split peas seasoned with turmeric and cloves and garnished with lemon wedges. Or use turmeric and a pinch of chile pepper to give a traditional Indian flavor to potato soup, cabbage, peas, cauliflower, or spinach.

Turmeric comes from the rhizome (a kind of underground stem) of *Curcuma longa,* a member of the ginger family. Adventurer Marco Polo brought news of turmeric to the West in the thirteenth century, but the spice had been in use in Asia for more than 2,500 years before that, appearing in ancient Sanskrit texts as *haridra,* from which its Indian name, *haldi,* derives. Turmeric has long held sacred meaning in Hinduism, in which it is associated with the sun and the deity Vishnu, and its bright yellow-orange color symbolizes fertility and prosperity. Ayurvedic medicine employs turmeric as an anti-inflammatory and antiaging compound, and modern studies have shown turmeric's positive effect on memory in the elderly.

Turmeric gives curry its signature golden color. Today, India produces more than 90 percent of the world's supply of this dazzling yellow spice. Originally concocted by British families nostalgic for the tastes of Indian cooking, curries and turmeric are popular wherever British and Indian immigrants have settled, and have taken on local savor in each place ("turmerick pudding" was served in London in 1704).

In India, fiery Madras curry powder for lamb and pork mixes turmeric, coriander, cumin, black pepper, ginger, and chili powder. Meanwhile, a world away, West Indian curry includes turmeric, coriander, cumin, black pepper, ginger, anise seed, cinnamon, and fenugreek. Everywhere, curried lamb, chicken, and beef are savory favorites, but try curry as a festive flavoring for shrimp or shellfish or to perk up vegetables.

Use turmeric with discretion—too much can make foods bitter.

Festive Zests

Orange and lemon zests' bewitching fragrances and bright tastes perk up the flavor of custards, pies, sherbets, preserves and marmalades, zucchini and pumpkin breads, cakes, and pastries. But zests are nothing if not versatile: as Latin American and Mediterranean cooks have long known, orange and lemon zests surprise, jolt, and enliven savory dishes as well. Soups, stews, meats, poultry, fish and shellfish, sauces, and vegetables sparkle with the delectable quality zests bring to food. The almost magical flavor-enhancing quality of zests makes them a delicious and natural substitute for salt. They ornament any flavor, and their confetti colors bring a festive note to any table.

Zests will add depth, color, and texture to any recipe that calls for orange or lemon juice. But because the flavor of zests' essential oils is more complex than juice and less acidic, zests can also work a more subtle magic, adding delicate hints of orange or lemon flavor where the sharpness of juice would be out of place.

Lemons and oranges are part of a single species, *Citrus,* that includes limes, tangerines, grapefruits, and mandarin oranges, among others. Their probable ancestor, the citron, was known in Roman times, but the history of citrus goes back thousands of years before that to Southeast Asia. From there, the luscious fruits spread along trade routes to North Africa and around the Mediterranean.

Lemons and Persian bitter oranges had reached Sicily by the Middle Ages; and Muslim settlers of the Umayyad dynasty cultivated citrus in the Iberian peninsula along with pomegranates, eggplants, artichokes, almonds, sugarcane, figs, peaches, and grapes. Today, descendants of those orange trees perfume the cool courtyard of Seville's cathedral, a former medieval mosque.

By the Renaissance, oranges and lemons had become status fruits: the Medici of Florence adopted the orange as their symbol, and it appears in paintings they commissioned, such as Botticelli's *Primavera.* Orangeries where citrus was grown indoors later became popular in affluent homes—Louis XIV had one, as did George Washington later on.

After 1492, oranges and lemons went to sea with Spanish explorers, who brought citrus to the Americas. The Spaniards introduced the sweet orange, *Citrus sinensis,* to Florida at their settlement at St. Augustine, beginning one of the world's great agricultural love stories. Missionary friars later spread the fruit to Arizona and California, at that time part of Mexico.

Orange zest and coriander

Today, Brazil is the world's top producer of oranges, while the United States, Mexico, and Italy lead in the production of lemons.

Fold lemon zest and capers into soft tangy cheese for a delectable spread, or try orange zest and a mild blue cheese. Orange or lemon zest, ginger, and yogurt make a savory, low-calorie dip for veggies. Stir zests into mayonnaise and use to dip asparagus, to transform chicken or tuna salad, or to update classics like Niçoise or Waldorf salads. Or sprinkle zest over a salad of baby greens or watercress.

Cosmopolitan, kir, or martini, anyone? Try a pinch of zest in your favorite cocktail, in sweet Belgian-style beers, or to flavor vodka or an impromptu sangria. And remember, orange zest works well in savory or sweet recipes that call for cognac or orange-based liqueurs such as Grand Marnier, Triple Sec, or Cointreau.

Make up some orange- or lemon-zest sugar and keep it on hand for adding sweet citrus sparkle wherever it's needed. Stir 1 teaspoon lemon or orange zest (or a little of each) into ⅓ cup sugar and store in an airtight container, allowing the flavors to blend for a week. Sprinkle it on fruit, pancakes or French toast, oatmeal, or granola— you'll want to be the first down to breakfast! Dust over angel food cake or pound cake, spoon onto custard, chocolate mousse, or pudding, or sprinkle a bit over whipped cream or crème fraîche.

To make a sweet citrus glaze for baked goods, moisten confectioners' sugar with orange or lemon juice, sprinkle in orange or lemon zest (or both), and spread or drizzle on sweet rolls, cupcakes, cookies, coconut bars, or angel food cake. Try lemon or orange zest mixed into the crust of fruit pies and tarts (plum, apple, and berry especially).

Substitutions: 1 teaspoon of dried orange or lemon zest can be used in place of 2 tablespoons of fresh lemon juice in many recipes. Or use orange or lemon zest in place of chopped candied peel for a fresh-tasting difference.

Lemon Zest

Lemon zest shines in sweet breads and pastries, custards, or apple pie, and, of course, it excels with seafood and chicken. Other affinities include broccoli, Brussels sprouts, asparagus, all kinds of green vegetables, and walnuts. Toss succulent green olives in olive oil, lemon zest, oregano, or thyme for an appetizer. Or follow the Latin American lead and add lemon zest and a squeeze of lemon juice to give piquancy to *caldo de pollo* or other savory soups.

Lemon zest adds intricacy to the classic Mediterranean marinade of lemon juice, olive oil, rosemary, salt, and pepper. Use on chicken or swordfish.

Orange Zest

In 1587, oranges were rare enough in the north that most of his readers had to take his word for it. We know, though, that orange zest's flavor is round and full and its fragrance heady. Orange zest goes especially well with beef, ham, and pork. Orange zest complements sweet potato or pumpkin, whether as the dinner vegetable or baked into a tasty pie. Orange zest is a natural with the flavors of almonds, coconut, mint, ginger, and chocolate. Try adding orange zest to brownies or chocolate cake batters. Or sprinkle onto vanilla ice cream for a taste reminiscent of childhood summer treats.

Orange zest, caraway, and fennel seed are the traditional flavorings of rich, dark Swedish rye bread.

Breakfast

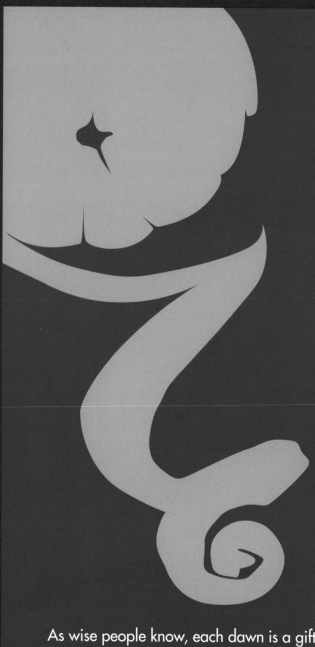

As wise people know, each dawn is a gift, a fresh start filled with possibility. That's as true of our food as of the other aspects of our lives. We like to start the morning with a burst of flavor, just to remind us to seek out a little adventure each day.

We all have our breakfast favorites, whether it's a bowl of hot oatmeal, pancakes, waffles, a slice of quick bread, or a dish that features that all-purpose nutritional powerhouse, the lovely egg. In this chapter, we offer a lot of familiar recipes, each of them with a flavorful twist that will wake up your taste buds and get you ready for a brand-new day.

Spiced Yogurt

· ·

If you need a demonstration of spice enlightenment, yogurt is a good place to start. Stir in a teaspoon of cinnamon and half that of ginger, give it a stir, and an ordinary food becomes memorable. It's also versatile. With breakfast granola or pound cake at lunch or dinner, this yogurt is delicious and healthy. This recipe calls for vanilla yogurt, but if you prefer less sweetness, it works well with plain yogurt, especially a rich, creamy, Greek-style yogurt.

2 cups vanilla yogurt
1 teaspoon ground cinnamon
½ teaspoon ground ginger

Combine the yogurt, cinnamon, and ginger in a medium bowl and mix well. Serve the yogurt immediately or store in the refrigerator in an airtight container.

Makes 2 cups

fun fact

The Roman writer Herodotus thought cinnamon came from mountain crags of Ethiopia, where it was furtively harvested from the nests of huge, dangerous birds. Pliny laughed at this and claimed Arab traders invented the story to conceal the real source and maintain the fantastic prices Romans were willing to pay for the spice.

Spiced Yogurt and Granola Parfait

Think of the meals that linger in your memory, and they probably won't be the ones with fancy menus or exotic ingredients. More often, you'll find yourself longing for the simple but delicious foods of a meal with family or friends. This parfait is a simple concoction—granola, fruit, and yogurt—but it's a lovely way to start a special day. Sara likes to make it in her mother's crystal iced-tea goblets—the ones considered "too good to use"—and serve it on holiday mornings.

3 cups Spiced Granola (page 37)
2 cups Spiced Yogurt (page 29)
3 cups assorted berries (such as raspberries,
    blackberries, blueberries, or strawberries)

In each of 4 footed parfait or ice cream glasses, scoop ¼ cup of granola. On top of the granola, layer ¼ cup of yogurt, and ¼ cup of berries. Repeat layering using ¼ cup each of the granola, yogurt, and berries. Top each parfait with ¼ cup each of the granola and berries and serve immediately.

Makes 4 parfaits

Smart spice? Studies indicate that a whiff of cinnamon can help improve concentration and make you more alert.

Toasting Pecans or Walnuts

Place a rack in the middle of the oven and preheat the oven to 350°F.
Spread the chopped nuts on a baking sheet and toast for about 5
minutes or just until the nuts begin to darken in color or you begin to
notice a toasty smell. There is a fine line between toasting nuts and
burning them, so pay attention!

Banana Muffins Spices and Orange Zest

There's something scrumptious about a muffin, especially one that takes the familiar taste of banana bread, spices it up, then gives you that crusty top that makes muffins so addictive. You can drop a spice or add a different one, but this is the combination that had all Sara's friends begging for another batch.

3 to 4 overripe bananas
1 cup sugar
1 teaspoon dried orange zest
1 teaspoon ground coriander
1 teaspoon ground ginger
1 teaspoon ground cloves
1 teaspoon ground cinnamon
2 large eggs
8 tablespoons (1 stick) butter, melted and cooled
1½ cups all-purpose flour
½ cup old-fashioned rolled oats
1 teaspoon baking soda
1 teaspoon salt
**1 cup nuts (we prefer walnuts or pecans), chopped,
     toasted, and cooled**

Preheat the oven to 350°F and grease a 12-cup muffin tin.

Mash the bananas, sugar, orange zest, and spices together. Gently whisk the eggs, pour in the melted butter, and add to the banana mixture. Sift the flour, oats, baking soda, and salt together and add to the banana mixture, stirring only until the ingredients are combined. Do not overstir. Fold in the nuts.

Fill the muffin tins and bake the muffins for 30 minutes, or until a knife inserted into the center of a muffin comes out clean. Remove the muffins from the oven and cool them on a wire rack.

Makes 1 dozen muffins

Oat-Nut Cluster Granola Cups

· ·

These granola "cupcakes" put commercial granola bars to shame. Healthy, handy, and altogether yummy, they are perfect for breakfast-on-the-go, for lunch bags, or for a midafternoon snack.

2 cups old-fashioned rolled oats
½ cup chopped pecans
½ cup sliced almonds
½ cup raw pumpkin seeds
½ cup honey
¼ cup firmly packed brown sugar
2 tablespoons unsalted butter
2 teaspoons vanilla
1 teaspoon ground cinnamon
1 teaspoon ground allspice
1 teaspoon dried orange zest
½ teaspoon kosher salt
6 ounces (1⅓ cups) sweetened dried cranberries
½ cup flaked coconut, preferably sweetened

Preheat the oven to 350°F. Spread the oats, pecans, almonds, and pumpkin seeds in a single layer on a jelly roll pan. Toast the oat and nut mixture in the oven for 15 minutes, stirring occasionally.

While the oat and nut mixture is toasting, combine the honey, brown sugar, butter, vanilla, cinnamon, allspice, orange zest, and salt in a medium saucepan. Cook the honey mixture over medium heat, stirring frequently, until the sugar has dissolved.

Decrease the oven heat to 300°F. Add the toasted oat and nut mixture to the honey mixture and stir to combine. Add the cranberries and coconut and stir until the granola mixture is thoroughly mixed. Evenly divide the granola mixture among 12 standard-size nonstick muffin cups. Press the granola mixture lightly into the cups and bake for 25 minutes. Remove the granola cups from the oven and allow them to cool completely before removing them from the pan. Store the granola cups in an airtight container.

Makes 12 granola cups

Variation: Use a mini-muffin pan and make 24 smaller treats. Follow the same directions, but decrease the final baking time, checking the cups after 10 to 12 minutes.

Enlightened Oatmeal

● ●

If you're going to eat oatmeal, why settle for the instant stuff? We'd always loved steel-cut oatmeal but rarely had time to cook it—until we learned a very sensible shortcut from our friend Mary. Just before bedtime, she sets out her pot, adds oats and water, and lets the oats soak overnight. The next morning, the oatmeal needs only 10 to 15 minutes to reach its best consistency, chewy but nutty.

We added the enlightenment to the equation—a teaspoon of any spice that strikes your fancy. Let that soak with the oats and you're bound to love your breakfast. There's an added bonus. With the spices for flavor, you'll need a lot less sugar—maybe none at all.

1 cup steel-cut oats
1 to 2 teaspoons of spice (choose your favorite:
    cinnamon, green cardamom, allspice, anise seed,
    cloves, ginger, **or any combination you like)**
4 cups water

Place the oats, spice, and water in a large pot before bedtime so that the mixture can soak for several hours. Next morning, bring the mixture to a boil and cook the oats, stirring frequently, for 10 to 15 minutes, or until the oats are chewy but retain a nutty consistency. Do not overcook.

Serve with buttermilk (traditional in Ireland) or regular milk. Add a touch of brown sugar or maple syrup if you like it a little sweeter.

Serves 4 to 6

Even Quicker Enlightened Oatmeal

For mornings when you don't have time for steel-cut oatmeal—or didn't have a chance to soak the oats overnight—old-fashioned rolled oats are a fine substitute.

2 cups water
⅛ teaspoon salt
1 cup old-fashioned rolled oats
¼ cup dried fruit (raisins, dates, cranberries)
1 teaspoon ground spice (choose from cinnamon, green cardamom, allspice, anise seed, cloves, nutmeg, **or any combination you like)**

In a medium-size saucepan, bring the water and salt to a boil over medium heat. Add the oats, dried fruit, and spice and cook, stirring occasionally, for 5 to 7 minutes, or until the oatmeal reaches your desired consistency. Serve with milk, if desired, or add a touch of brown sugar or maple syrup if you like it a little sweeter.

Serves 2

Whole cloves look a lot like little nails, so it's no surprise that the name comes from clavus, the Latin word for "nail." The Chinese word for clove translates as "nail spice."

fun fact

Cinnamon is packed with antioxidants and may also have a role in regulating insulin. In traditional medicine it's reputed to stimulate the appetite and relieve coughs and colds. This versatile spice also has a proven antimicrobial effect.

Spiced Granola (with) Coconut and Almonds

It's easy to reach for granola in the cereal aisle, and there are some very good commercially made brands on the market. But once you discover how easy it is to mix and toast your own—and how much fun it is to tweak it to your own particular preferences— you'll likely be a convert to the homemade kind.

We think the following recipe has it all. It's easy and fun to make. With whole grains and flax seed, it provides a nutritional punch. Best of all, it's delicious. Katie likes to keep a bowl around to nibble on all morning. The recipe calls for sweetened coconut, but unsweetened is fine, too.

½ cup firmly packed brown sugar
8 tablespoons (1 stick) unsalted butter
1 teaspoon ground cinnamon
1 teaspoon ground green cardamom
1 teaspoon ground ginger
1 teaspoon dried orange zest
1 teaspoon vanilla
1 teaspoon salt
2 cups old-fashioned rolled oats
1 cup flaked coconut, preferably sweetened
1 cup sliced almonds
1 cup chopped pecans
½ cup whole flax seed

Preheat the oven to 350°F. Combine the brown sugar, butter, cinnamon, cardamom, ginger, orange zest, vanilla, and salt in a small saucepan. Heat the mixture over medium heat, stirring frequently, until the sugar has dissolved.

Combine the oats, coconut, almonds, pecans, and flax seed in a large bowl. Add the brown sugar mixture and toss until the oat and nut mixture is evenly coated. Spread the granola in a single layer on a jelly roll pan. Bake the granola for 10 to 15 minutes, stirring every 5 minutes. Remove the granola from the oven and allow to cool before serving. Store the granola in an airtight container for up to 2 weeks.

Makes 4 cups

Warm, Spicy Grapefruit

Grapefruit has long been a wintertime breakfast favorite. Add a little sugar and spice and it becomes an elegant treat.

6 tablespoons firmly packed brown sugar
1 teaspoon ground cumin
1 teaspoon ground cinnamon
3 red grapefruit, halved

Preheat the broiler and coat a baking sheet with nonstick spray. Mix the brown sugar, cumin, and cinnamon together and divide evenly over each grapefruit half.

Place the grapefruit, cut side up, on the prepared sheet and broil for 3 minutes or until bubbly. Remove from the oven and serve immediately.

Serves 6

Note: The sugar mixture is also good over sliced bananas or thinly sliced apples. Broil the bananas 3 minutes and the apples 4 to 5 minutes.

Gingerbread Waffles

Waffles are a special breakfast treat, reserved for mornings when there is enough time to mix the batter and wait for the waffle iron to heat. Then comes the hardest part, especially for kids—smelling the aroma while waiting for the waffle to cook.

This recipe makes the wait even harder, as the scent of spices wafts through the kitchen. If you like waffles, this recipe will give you a new reason to heat up the iron. If you like gingerbread, it will give you a new way to get your fix. Waffles with gingerbread spices—now, there's a breakfast to love.

2 cups all-purpose flour
1 tablespoon baking
  powder
1 teaspoon baking soda
½ teaspoon salt
2 teaspoons ground ginger
2 teaspoons ground
  cinnamon
1 teaspoon ground cloves

1 teaspoon dried orange zest
3 eggs, separated
8 tablespoons (1 stick) butter,
  melted
1 cup milk
½ cup firmly packed dark brown
  sugar
½ cup molasses

Preheat the waffle iron. Sift together the flour, baking powder, baking soda, salt, ginger, cinnamon, cloves, and orange zest into a large mixing bowl. In a small bowl, whisk together the 3 egg yolks and the butter until thoroughly combined. Whisk the milk, brown sugar, and molasses into the egg mixture. Add the egg mixture to the flour mixture and stir until just combined.

In a separate bowl, beat the remaining 3 egg whites until soft peaks form. Fold the egg whites into the batter. Coat the waffle iron with nonstick cooking spray or brush with flavorless oil. Pour enough batter in the iron to just cover the waffle grid, close, and cook according to the manufacturer's instructions until golden brown. Remove the waffle and repeat until all the batter is used. Serve the waffles immediately or keep warm for up to 20 minutes in a 200°F oven.

Makes 4 cups of batter, or 6 regular waffles

Notes:

Serve this waffle with your favorite syrup, or with Ginger-Allspice Applesauce (page 42). Pair it with lemon curd or berries and whipped cream for an elegant dessert.

These waffles freeze well, so make extra for mornings when there's no time to heat the waffle iron.

Spiced Pancakes

• •

There's something about certain spice combinations that create an intoxicating sum of the individual parts. This combination of ginger, cinnamon, and cloves is one of them. You'll never be able to eat plain pancakes again. Even better, you'll love the pancakes as much as—maybe even more than—the sweet stuff you add on top.

1 large egg
¼ cup firmly packed brown sugar
1 cup milk
½ stick unsalted butter, melted and cooled
1 cup old-fashioned rolled oats
1 cup all-purpose flour
1 teaspoon baking soda
1 teaspoon salt
1 teaspoon ground ginger
1 teaspoon ground cinnamon
1 teaspoon ground cloves

Heat a griddle over medium heat. In a medium bowl, stir the egg and brown sugar together, then add the milk and butter. In a small bowl, whisk together the oats, flour, baking soda, salt, and spices. Add the oat mixture to the egg mixture and stir until combined.

Brush the griddle with vegetable oil and drop enough batter to make 4-inch pancakes, about ¼ cup each. Cook until bubbles appear on the surface and the undersides are brown, about 2 minutes. Flip the pancakes with the spatula and cook until the undersides become golden brown and the pancakes are cooked through, about 2 minutes.

The pancakes are great with fresh fruit and maple syrup, or with Ginger-Allspice Applesauce (page 42).

Makes about 14 pancakes

fun fact

Cloves have mild anesthetic and antimicrobial properties and in the past were used to treat toothaches. Even today, preparations containing cloves are used in dentistry, as mouthwashes, and for sore throats.

Ginger-Allspice Applesauce

When you see how easy it is to make your own applesauce—and how much fun to vary it with different kinds of apples and different spices—you'll wonder why you ever fell for the commercial stuff. Don't be fooled by thinking only a few kinds of apples are good for cooking. We like using a variety of apples—Winesaps, McIntosh, Galas, and others—and, of course, a variety of spices.

This sauce is equally good with waffles and pancakes in the morning or pork chops and gingerbread later in the day.

12 medium apples
¾ cup apple cider or apple juice
1 teaspoon ground allspice
1 teaspoon ground ginger
1 teaspoon dried lemon zest

Peel, core, and slice each apple into 8 wedges. Place the apple wedges in a 3-quart heavy pot over medium heat. Add the cider or juice, allspice, ginger, and lemon zest. Simmer gently for 20 to 30 minutes, or until the apples are tender. Remove from the heat and thoroughly mash the apples.

Serves 6

Allspice is the berry of an evergreen tree. The tree will not flower outside the Western Hemisphere, but it thrives in Jamaica, where most of the world's allspice is grown.

Blueberry Coffee Cake

Coffee always tastes better when there's a good coffee cake around. So does tea! With blueberries, walnuts, and a gentle dose of spice and zest, this cake makes the morning shine.

8 tablespoons (1 stick) unsalted butter, at room temperature
¾ cup sugar
2 eggs
1½ teaspoons vanilla
1¼ cups plus 1 tablespoon all-purpose flour
1 teaspoon baking powder
½ teaspoon salt
¼ teaspoon baking soda
½ cup buttermilk
1 cup fresh blueberries or frozen, thawed, and well drained
⅓ cup firmly packed brown sugar
2 teaspoons ground cinnamon
2 teaspoons dried lemon zest
1 cup chopped walnuts

Preheat the oven to 350°F and grease and flour an 8-inch square or round baking pan. Cream the butter and sugar in a large mixing bowl until light and fluffy. In a small bowl, whisk together the eggs and vanilla. Add the egg mixture to the butter mixture and beat until the batter is combined.

Sift together 1¼ cups of the flour, the baking powder, salt, and baking soda into a small bowl. Gradually mix ½ of the flour mixture and ½ of the buttermilk into the dry ingredients. Add the remaining flour mixture and the remaining buttermilk and stir until both are incorporated into the mixture. In a small bowl, toss the blueberries in the remaining 1 tablespoon of flour. Carefully fold the blueberries into the batter.

Combine the brown sugar, cinnamon, and lemon zest in a small bowl. Pour ½ of the batter into the prepared pan. Evenly sprinkle the walnuts over the batter. Sprinkle ½ of the brown sugar mixture evenly over the nuts. Cover the nuts with the remaining batter and evenly sprinkle with the remaining brown sugar mixture. Bake for 45 minutes, or until a toothpick inserted in the center comes out clean.

Makes 1 (8-inch square or round) coffee cake

Pepperoni Spinach Frittata

Elegant but easy, a frittata is perfect for those special-occasion breakfasts. The basil and anise seed complement the pepperoni, but feel free to vary the spices. Instead of basil and anise seed, try oregano and fennel seed—or your own favorite combination.

5 eggs
1 teaspoon basil
1 teaspoon anise seed
¼ teaspoon coarse black pepper
Pinch of salt
½ cup shredded mozzarella cheese
½ cup frozen chopped spinach, thawed and
    squeezed dry
¼ cup sliced pepperoni, cut into strips
¼ cup freshly grated Parmesan cheese
2 tablespoons olive oil
1 cup diced yellow onion
1 red bell pepper, diced
1 clove garlic, minced

Preheat the broiler. Beat together the eggs, basil, anise seed, black pepper, and salt in a medium bowl. Stir in the mozzarella, spinach, pepperoni, and Parmesan cheese.

Heat the oil in an ovenproof, nonstick medium skillet over medium heat. Stir in the onion and bell pepper and sauté until tender, about 5 minutes. Add the garlic and sauté for 1 minute.

Pour the egg mixture into the skillet and stir to combine the eggs and vegetables. Decrease the heat to low and cook the frittata until the egg mixture has set on the bottom and begins to set on top, about 5 minutes. Transfer the skillet to the broiler and continue cooking until the frittata is set, 3 to 4 minutes. A traditional frittata is not browned. Loosen the edges of the frittata with a spatula, slide the frittata onto a plate, and serve immediately.

Serves 4

Breakfast Tostada

• •

There's such a thing as a chile pepper morning—when you need some real tingle on the tongue. That's when you know it's a tostada morning, complete with all the toppings. This is a great brunch dish and perfect for company. Be prepared to double—or triple—the recipe, because they'll be coming back for more.

> **4 teaspoons canola or other mild-tasting oil**
> **4 (6-inch) corn tortillas**
> **½ cup shredded cheddar cheese**
> **4 eggs**
> **½ to 1 teaspoon ground** ancho chile pepper
> **Kosher salt**
> **1 (15-ounce) can black beans, drained and warmed**
> **Diced tomatoes or salsa, for topping**
> **Spiced Guacamole (page 85), for topping**
> **Cumin-Cilantro Sour Cream Dip (page 87), for topping**

Heat 1 teaspoon of the oil in a small skillet over medium-high heat. Place one of the tortillas in the oil and fry the tortilla until it is golden brown. Flip the tortilla over and sprinkle with 2 tablespoons of the cheese. Decrease the heat to low and crack a single egg over the melting cheese. Season the egg with ⅓ to ¼ teaspoon of the ancho chile pepper and a pinch of salt. Cover the pan with a lid and cook until the white of the egg just begins to set, 3 to 4 minutes. Carefully flip the tortilla over and heat until the egg is thoroughly cooked, 3 to 4 minutes. Place the tostada on a plate tortilla side down. Prepare three additional tostadas using the remaining oil, tortillas, cheese, eggs, ancho chile pepper, and salt.

Top each tostada with the beans, tomatoes or salsa, guacamole, and sour cream as desired. Serve immediately.

Serves 4

Note: You can substitute mild chile pepper for the ancho.

fun fact

Chile pepper is reputed to relieve arthritis, revive a flagging love life, and cure intestinal worms. Scientists note that preliminary studies indicate chile pepper may help regulate the body's production of insulin.

Spicy Southwestern Quiche

. . . .

Let's face it: a quiche can be bland—sort of like a dull room calling out for some color. Cumin, coriander, and chile pepper lend a splash of Southwest flavor to this dish. It's perfect for a weekend brunch—if you're willing to share.

Basic Pie Crust Dough (page 169)
made with ground coriander
6 eggs
1 teaspoon ground cumin
1 teaspoon ground ancho chile pepper
1 teaspoon ground coriander
1 teaspoon salt
½ teaspoon garlic powder
1 cup heavy cream
1½ cups shredded Monterey Jack cheese
½ cup corn, fresh or frozen and thawed
⅓ cup diced green bell pepper
⅓ cup diced red bell pepper
¼ cup diced red onion
¼ cup chopped fresh cilantro

Preheat the oven to 350°F. Line a 9-inch pie plate with the pie crust dough, trim the edges, and finish as desired. Bake the crust for 5 minutes.

While the crust is baking, beat together the eggs, cumin, ancho chile, coriander, salt, and garlic powder in a large mixing bowl. Beat in the heavy cream. Stir in the cheese, corn, bell peppers, onion, and cilantro. Pour the egg mixture into the partially baked crust and bake for 1 hour, or until the filling is browned and set. Let the quiche cool for 15 minutes before serving.

Makes 1 (9-inch) quiche

In ancient Rome, cumin symbolized avarice. Toga-clad cheapskates were scorned as "cumin splitters" and were said to "eat cumin." The spice's association with excessive thrift earned Roman emperor and Stoic philosopher Marcus Aurelius the nickname "Cumin."

Salads, Soups, and Sandwiches

We remember when the noontime meal was "dinner" and the table was groaning with food, including plenty of fresh-picked, homegrown vegetables. These days, we'd need a siesta to eat like that in the middle of the day. Alas, our schedules don't allow for that luxury.

But a smaller, simpler meal doesn't have to mean a plain and boring meal—or one so hurried we don't have time to savor the flavor. We think that's one of the problems in our society—not taking time to enjoy our food. Maybe that's because too much of the food we eat is drab and flavorless.

We believe that lunch, like every meal, should be good for you and good to eat. These lunch recipes prove that simple food can be deliciously satisfying, surprisingly different from ordinary lunch food, and not difficult to make.

We're big on salads, soups, and sandwiches. Here you'll find some of our favorites and, no doubt, some of your own. We've tweaked them, of course, adding vibrant flavors from our favorite trove of herbs and spices.

Try them, and you might find ways to turn some of your old recipes into new favorite foods. And, of course, feel free to use these recipes at other meals as well. These salads and soups make excellent starters for dinner.

Strawberry Salad

with

Balsamic Cinnamon Vinaigrette

• •

Strawberries can make any food seem special, as this salad demonstrates. Serve it with the cinnamon vinaigrette and people who normally avoid "rabbit food" will want to lick their plates.

7 to 8 cups spring mix baby greens
1 pint fresh strawberries, stemmed and quartered
1 avocado, sliced
½ small red onion, thinly sliced
½ cup chopped pecans, toasted (see page 32)
½ cup Balsamic Cinnamon Vinaigrette (recipe follows)

Combine the greens, strawberries, avocado, onion, and pecans in a large salad bowl. Gently toss the salad with the dressing and serve immediately.

Makes 4 to 6 side salads or 2 full salads

Balsamic Cinnamon Vinaigrette

Cinnamon is a common flavor in American food, but in a salad it comes as a sweet surprise. Once you see what this charming vinaigrette can do for strawberry salad, you'll have a new reason to eat your greens.

¼ cup balsamic vinegar
1 tablespoon sugar
1 teaspoon ground cinnamon
½ teaspoon salt
¼ cup olive oil

Whisk together the vinegar, sugar, cinnamon, and salt in a small bowl. Add the oil in a slow, steady steam, whisking constantly, until blended. Serve immediately.

Makes ½ cup

Waldorf Salad Cardamom Candied Walnuts

• •

When fall brings fresh apples, it's a shame not to enjoy them every way you can. We have always been fond of apple salad, but with the addition of our tasty Cardamom Candied Walnuts, our affection for this lovely salad has moved up a few notches. Pair Waldorf salad with creamy Carrot Soup with Coriander (page 59) for a satisfying lunch.

¼ **cup mayonnaise**
¼ **cup sour cream**
1½ **teaspoons freshly squeezed lemon juice**
1 **teaspoon dried** lemon zest
½ **teaspoon sugar**
2 **medium Granny Smith apples, cored, cut into ½-inch**
   cubes
¾ **cup red seedless grapes, halved**
¾ **cup thinly sliced celery**
¾ **cup Cardamom Candied Walnuts (page 79), chopped**
Lettuce leaves, for serving

Whisk together the mayonnaise, sour cream, lemon juice, lemon zest, and sugar in a medium bowl. Stir in the apples, grapes, celery, and walnuts and gently toss the salad until evenly coated. Serve the salad on a bed of fresh lettuce.

Makes 4 cups

fun fact

Although nineteenth-century British sailors were nicknamed "limeys," it was actually lemons that saved them from the dreaded scurvy.

Toasting Almonds

Place a rack in the middle of the oven and preheat the oven to 350°F. Spread the sliced almonds evenly on a baking sheet and toast for about 5 minutes or until the almonds just begin to turn golden brown and fragrant. There is a fine line between toasting nuts and burning them, so pay attention and remove them from the oven as soon as they get that toasty smell.

Spinach Salad (with) Blackberry Vinaigrette

● ●

We could make a meal on tender baby spinach leaves, even without the added appeal of mandarin oranges, avocado, and almonds. Dress it all in a zesty blackberry vinaigrette, and you've got a sensational lunch or an impressive addition to the dinner table.

7 to 8 cups baby spinach
1 (6-ounce) can mandarin oranges, drained
1 avocado, peeled, pitted, and sliced
½ small red onion, thinly sliced
½ cup sliced almonds, toasted
¾ cup Blackberry Vinaigrette (recipe follows)

Combine the spinach, mandarin oranges, avocado, onion, and almonds in a large salad bowl. Gently toss the salad with the blackberry vinaigrette and serve immediately.

Makes 4 to 6 side salads or 2 full salads

What do grease monkeys and the nobles of ancient China have in common? Both care for their hands with oranges. Chinese ladies once carried oranges so the delicate oils would perfume their hands. Today, these same oils put the grease-cutting horsepower into modern mechanics' hand cleaners (and they still smell nice).

Blackberry Vinaigrette

Mellow orange zest is the perfect counterpoint for plump, juicy blackberries with their tart-sweet appeal. This vinaigrette shows how a well-chosen pairing of fruit and zest can yield a delightful balance.

½ cup blackberries
¼ cup white balsamic vinegar
1½ tablespoons sugar
1 teaspoon dried orange zest
¼ teaspoon salt
¼ cup olive oil

In a small mixing bowl, mash the blackberries with a whisk until they are crushed and have released their juice. Whisk in the vinegar, sugar, orange zest, and salt. Add the oil in a slow, steady steam, whisking constantly, until blended. Serve immediately.

Makes ¾ cup

Rosemary-Crusted Steak Salad Warm Balsamic Vinaigrette

Steak salad makes an elegant and filling midday meal. Our warm balsamic vinaigrette enhances the pan juices and pairs perfectly with the herb-crusted steaks. We love these steaks sliced and served as a salad, but they're also delicious as a dinner entrée.

4 (5-ounce) beef tenderloin
  steaks, about 1 inch
  thick
1½ teaspoons black
  pepper
1 teaspoon rosemary
1 teaspoon marjoram
¾ teaspoon kosher salt

1 tablespoon olive oil
1 tablespoon butter
1 cup balsamic vinegar
2 tablespoons soy sauce
4 cloves garlic, minced
8 ounces arugula

Pat the steaks dry. Combine the pepper, rosemary, marjoram, and salt in a small bowl. Sprinkle the spice mixture evenly over both sides of each steak, pressing the spices into the meat.

Heat the oil and butter in a medium skillet over medium heat. Add the steaks and cook, turning once, until the steaks reach desired doneness. Transfer the steaks to a cutting board and let stand, loosely covered with aluminum foil, for 10 minutes. (The steaks will continue to cook as they stand.)

While the steak is resting, warm the remaining pan drippings over medium-high heat. Pour in the vinegar to deglaze the pan and, using a wooden spoon, scrape the bottom of the pan to dislodge any brown bits. Add the soy sauce and garlic and reduce the vinaigrette, stirring continually, until it thickens, about 5 minutes. Stir in any meat drippings that have collected on the cutting board.

Cut the steaks into ¼-inch-thick slices. Divide the arugula onto four plates and arrange the steak slices on the beds of arugula. Drizzle the warm vinaigrette over the salads and serve immediately.

Serves 4

Legend has it that the Virgin Mary, resting with the infant Jesus on her flight from Herod's soldiers, draped her cloak over a rosemary bush. According to the tale, the flowers ever afterward bloomed a delicate blue.

Carrot Soup with Coriander

The bright, lemony notes of coriander are a perfect complement for carrots. This appealing soup is delicious with only the coriander, but a teaspoon of turmeric adds a warm, earthy undertone. Feel free to substitute half-and-half or whole milk for the heavy cream.

1 tablespoon butter
1½ cups diced white or yellow onion
1 clove garlic, minced
1 tablespoon ground coriander
1 teaspoon ground turmeric (optional)
4 cups chicken broth
½ cup orange juice
5 medium carrots, peeled and sliced into rounds
1 medium potato, peeled and cut into cubes
¾ cup heavy cream
¼ cup chopped cilantro (optional)
Salt and black pepper

Melt the butter in a large saucepan over medium heat. Add the onion to the pan and sauté until tender, about 5 minutes. Stir in the garlic, coriander, and turmeric, if using, and cook for 1 minute. Add the chicken broth, orange juice, carrots, and potato and bring the soup to a boil. Simmer the soup over medium-high heat until the carrots are tender, about 30 minutes.

Using a blender or food processor, carefully purée the soup until smooth. Return the soup to the saucepan and stir in the cream. Warm the soup over medium heat until hot. Stir in the cilantro, if using, and season with salt and pepper to taste.

Makes 5 cups

fun fact

Turmeric turns bright red in the presence of alkaline substances and bright yellow when exposed to acidic solutions, so early chemists used "turmeric paper" to detect acidity or alkalinity. Traditional Indian textile crafters took advantage of this property to create brilliant silks and cottons in a range of yellows, oranges, and reds.

Creamy Tomato Basil Soup

If you're one of those people who think tomato soup is a bore, get ready to change your mind. This simple recipe makes a satisfying lunch and a tasty start to dinner.

Like any good soup recipe, it's a template. We love the addition of fennel seeds with the herbs, but you can skip the herbs altogether in favor of spices like coriander and cumin, or any combination that pleases you. If you're counting calories, feel free to substitute whole milk for the half-and-half.

> **1 teaspoon olive oil**
> **1 cup diced white or yellow onion**
> **1 tablespoon minced garlic**
> **2 (14½-ounce) cans diced tomatoes**
> **1 (15-ounce) can tomato sauce**
> **1 cup half-and-half**
> **3 teaspoons basil**
> **1 teaspoon oregano**
> **1 teaspoon fennel seed (optional)**
> **½ cup freshly grated Parmesan cheese,**
>   **plus additional for topping**
> **Salt and black pepper**
> **1 cup plain or garlic croutons (optional)**

Heat the olive oil in a large saucepan over medium heat. Add the onion to the pan and sauté until tender, about 5 minutes. Add the garlic and cook, stirring continually, for 1 minute. Add the diced tomatoes and tomato sauce and bring the soup to a boil. Decrease the heat to low and stir in the half-and-half, basil, oregano, and fennel seeds, if using, and cook, stirring occasionally, for 10 minutes.

Using a blender or food processor, carefully purée the soup until smooth. Return the puréed soup to the pan, and warm the soup over low heat until hot. Remove the saucepan from the heat, stir in the cheese, and season with salt and pepper to taste. Serve the soup topped with croutons, if using, and Parmesan cheese.

Serves 4

Variations: Omit the basil and oregano and use 1 teaspoon thyme, 1 teaspoon ground coriander, and 1 teaspoon ground cumin.

fun fact

In Tudor England, the gift of a pot of basil was considered a compliment to the recipient. Besides its popularity as a kitchen herb, it was believed to keep flies away.

Herbed Corn Chowder

• •

Who doesn't love a hearty chowder? The word, which always makes our mouths water, has been traced back to the Latin word *caldaria*, which originally referred to a place for warming things and later became the word for "cooking pot." Chowder can take many forms, but this one, featuring crunchy corn kernels and a trio of herbs, has become one of our favorites.

4 tablespoons (½ stick) butter	**1 tablespoon sugar**
1½ cups diced white or yellow onion	**1 teaspoon Worcestershire sauce**
¼ cup all-purpose flour	**1 teaspoon** dill weed
3 cups chicken broth	**1 teaspoon** marjoram
½ cup dry white wine	**½ teaspoon** sage
3 cups corn, fresh or frozen	**4 ounces cheddar cheese, grated**
2 cups heavy cream	**Salt and black pepper**

Melt the butter in a large saucepan over medium heat. Add the onion to the pan and sauté until tender, about 5 minutes. Add the flour and cook, stirring continually, for 3 minutes. Whisk in the broth and wine and cook, stirring continually, until the soup begins to thicken. Add in the corn, cream, sugar, Worcestershire, dill weed, marjoram, and sage and cook, stirring occasionally, for 15 minutes.

Using a slotted spoon, remove 3 cups of the corn and onion from the saucepan and set aside. Using a blender or food processor, carefully purée the remaining soup until smooth. Return the puréed soup to the pan, add the reserved corn and onion back to the soup, and warm the soup over medium heat until hot. Remove the saucepan from the heat, stir in the cheese, and season with salt and pepper to taste.

Makes approximately 6 cups

═══════════════════════════════════

Sage can be used as insect repellent, rubbed on the skin or placed in sachets to keep away moths and other marauders.

In sixteenth-century England, before conventional tea became the country's quintessential refreshing beverage, sage tea was a popular drink. Sage ale was brewed for those who preferred something stronger.

═══════════════════════════════════

Cheesy Spinach Lasagne Soup

• •

This hearty soup is a real crowd-pleaser. Best of all, it's much easier to make than traditional lasagne—and just as easy to enjoy.

1 pound ground Italian sausage
1 large onion (any variety), chopped
6 cloves garlic, minced
2 teaspoons basil
2 teaspoons oregano
1 teaspoon anise seed
4 cups chicken broth
1 (14½-ounce) can petite diced tomatoes
1 (8-ounce) can tomato sauce
1 cup mini farfalle pasta
2 packed cups fresh spinach, chopped
8 ounces fresh mozzarella cheese, diced
½ cup freshly shredded Parmesan cheese

Brown the sausage in a large saucepan over medium-high heat until crumbly. Remove the sausage from the pan and drain all but 1 tablespoon of the fat. Add the onion to the pan and sauté over medium heat until tender, about 5 minutes. Return the sausage to the pan, stir in the garlic, basil, oregano, and anise seed, and cook for 2 minutes. Add the chicken broth, diced tomatoes, and tomato sauce and bring to a boil over high heat. Stir in the pasta and cook, according to the manufacturer's recommended cook time, until the pasta is al dente. Remove the saucepan from the heat and stir in the spinach and mozzarella. Serve the soup immediately topped with Parmesan cheese.

Makes 8 cups

fun fact

Anise seeds were highly prized in ancient Rome. At the end of a feast, many Romans would consume the seeds to settle their stomachs and freshen their breath.

Pimento Cheese

Ah, pimento cheese, the "house pâté" of the South. There is no single way to make this iconic spread, and it's hard to go wrong. We've had it with dill weed, dill seed, caraway seed, and plenty of other spices and herbs. This version is one of our favorites, but we encourage you to try your own. (We are also partial to the spicier variation below.)

The dash of bourbon pays homage to the version of pimento cheese favored by Bill Neal, the North Carolina chef who elevated shrimp and grits from a Low Country fisherman's breakfast to haute cuisine.

For an easy and always satisfying sandwich, spread your favorite bread with pimento cheese. When there's time, we like to toast the bread first, which lends a lovely gooey quality to the spread. For an easy snack, spoon some "p.c.," as we like to call it, on the end of a celery stick.

8 ounces sharp cheddar cheese, grated
¼ cup freshly grated Parmesan cheese
6 ounces diced pimentos, drained
1 teaspoon dill weed
1 teaspoon ground coriander
1 teaspoon bourbon (optional)
¼ cup mayonnaise

In a medium bowl, combine the cheddar, Parmesan, pimentos, dill weed, coriander, and bourbon, if using, with a fork. Add the mayonnaise and stir, mashing the mixture with the fork, until mostly smooth. Cover and chill for 2 hours before serving.

Makes 2 cups

Variation: Replace the dill and coriander with 1 teaspoon of crushed ancho chile pepper and 1 teaspoon of ground cumin.

Chicken Salad on Croissant

· ·

We have lost count of the versions of chicken salad we have tasted and loved over the years. But this one has become our all-time favorite, with just the right mix of chicken and extra goodies like cranberries, pumpkin seeds, and—perhaps the star of the show— Cardamom Candied Walnuts. Gently spicing the mayonnaise with coriander and orange zest takes this chicken salad over the top. (You'll want to mix extra mayonnaise to spread on the sandwich—and you may want to keep extra on hand for other uses.)

This salad also works well with turkey. In fact, it's the perfect day-after-Thanksgiving sandwich.

½ cup mayonnaise, plus additional for spreading
1 teaspoon ground coriander
1 teaspoon dried orange zest
¼ teaspoon salt
¼ teaspoon black pepper
2 cups diced cooked chicken
½ cup Cardamom Candied Walnuts (page 79), chopped
½ cup sweetened dried cranberries
¼ cup finely diced yellow bell pepper
¼ cup finely diced celery
¼ cup finely diced red onion
2 tablespoons shelled sunflower or pumpkin seeds,
**   preferably roasted and salted**
4 croissants, halved horizontally

Whisk together the mayonnaise, coriander, orange zest, salt, and pepper in a medium bowl. Stir in the chicken, walnuts, cranberries, bell pepper, celery, onion, and seeds and gently toss the salad until evenly coated. Spread additional mayonnaise on the croissant halves if desired. Divide the chicken salad among the four croissants and serve.

Makes 4 sandwiches

Italian Grilled Cheese Sandwich

If a grilled cheese sandwich is your idea of comfort food, imagine taking it to the next level. It's still simple: just add a fresh tomato, embellish it with basil and homemade Italian dressing, and a simple sandwich becomes a meal to remember.

8 slices Italian bread, ½ inch thick
2 tablespoons Italian Dressing (recipe follows)
8 slices provolone cheese
1 medium tomato, thinly sliced
2 teaspoons basil

Brush one side of each slice of bread with Italian dressing. Place 4 of the bread slices dressing side down onto a work surface. Place 2 slices of cheese on each slice of bread and top with the sliced tomato. Evenly sprinkle basil over the tomato slices, ½ teaspoon of basil per sandwich. Top each sandwich with the remaining 4 bread slices, dressing side up. Heat a nonstick griddle or pan over medium heat for 2 minutes. Grill the sandwiches until the outside is golden brown and the cheese is just melted, 3 to 4 minutes per side. Cut the sandwiches in half and serve hot.

Makes 4 sandwiches

Italian Dressing

• •

This vinaigrette adds the perfect tang to our grilled cheese sandwich, but it's also a great way to dress a salad. In fact, it puts the bottled stuff to shame. You might want to keep a batch in the refrigerator.

¼ cup white wine vinegar
2 cloves garlic, minced
2 teaspoons minced shallots
1 teaspoon sugar
1 teaspoon mustard
1 teaspoon basil
½ teaspoon oregano
½ teaspoon salt
¼ cup olive oil

Whisk together the vinegar, garlic, shallots, sugar, mustard, basil, oregano, and salt in a small bowl. Add the oil in a slow, steady steam, whisking constantly, until blended.

Makes ½ cup

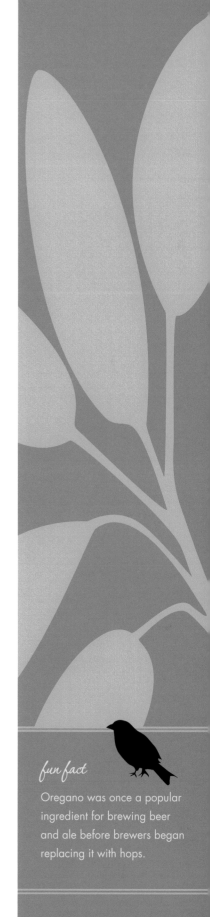

fun fact

Oregano was once a popular ingredient for brewing beer and ale before brewers began replacing it with hops.

TSP Reuben

• •

T (Thousand Island), S (Sauerkraut & Swiss), P (Pastrami)—now there's a formula for a sensational Reuben on rye, especially with a homemade Thousand Island Spread featuring the vibrant flavors of organic spices. Pair with a bowl of soup for a satisfying dose of comfort food.

2 tablespoons butter, at room temperature
8 slices rye bread
8 ounces thinly sliced Swiss cheese
1 pound thinly sliced pastrami, heated
1 cup well-drained sauerkraut, heated
½ cup Thousand Island Spread (recipe follows)

Butter one side of each slice of bread. Place 4 of the bread slices, butter side down, onto a large nonstick griddle or pan. Evenly divide the cheese slices between the 4 slices of bread. Divide the pastrami among the 4 sandwiches and arrange in an even layer on top of the cheese. Top each sandwich with ¼ cup of sauerkraut and arrange in an even layer on top of the pastrami. Spread 2 tablespoons of the Thousand Island Spread on the dry side of each of the remaining bread slices. Place the bread, spread side down, on top of the sauerkraut. Grill the sandwiches over medium-low heat until the outside is golden brown and the cheese is melted, 3 to 4 minutes per side. Cut the sandwiches in half and serve hot.

Makes 4 sandwiches

Thousand Island Spread

You've tasted the commercial stuff plenty of times. Now you see how easy it is to make your own—and how much better it can taste with fresh-tasting organic spices.

½ cup mayonnaise
¼ cup sweet pickle relish
2 tablespoons ketchup
1 teaspoon ground coriander
1 teaspoon ground allspice

Whisk together the mayonnaise, relish, ketchup, coriander, and allspice in a small bowl. Serve immediately or cover and store in the refrigerator for up to 4 weeks.

Makes ¾ cup

Appetizers and Snacks

The trick to a good appetizer is to tease your appetite without totally satisfying it. After all, we don't want to spoil dinner!

This collection of recipes features some old favorites, including two versions of deviled eggs, and some new contenders, such as our delightful pizza straws and skewered chicken nuggets with Middle Eastern flavors.

You'll also discover how easy it is to make your own guacamole or sour cream dip—and how tasty the homemade kind can be. Our spice-crusted cheese truffles will be a hit, and once you try this relatively simple but eminently satisfying treat, we hope you'll be inspired to come up with your own variations.

Pizza Straws

• •

Whether you need an appetizer or snack, or something to supplement a soup or salad, you'll love these cheesy pizza straws. They're also a perfect after-school snack.

1 (½-pound) sheet frozen puff pastry, thawed
1 egg
2 teaspoons water
1 cup finely shredded extra-sharp cheddar cheese
¼ cup finely and freshly grated Parmesan cheese
2 teaspoons anise seed
Coarse salt (optional)

Preheat the oven to 400°F. On a lightly floured surface, roll the pastry into a 14 by 12-inch rectangle. Whisk together the egg and water in a small bowl. Brush the pastry with the egg wash. Cut the pastry in half, forming two 14 by 6-inch rectangles. Evenly sprinkle the cheddar cheese, Parmesan cheese, and anise seeds over the top of one of the rectangles. Place the other rectangle, egg wash side down, on top of the cheese-topped rectangle. Gently roll the pastry with a rolling pin to make the layers adhere. Brush the top of the pastry with the egg wash and season with salt, if using. With a pastry wheel or sharp knife, cut the pastry into ¾-inch-wide strips.

Grease a baking sheet or line with parchment paper. Twist the strips and place 1 inch apart onto the baking sheet, pressing ends onto the sheet to keep the strips twisted. Bake for 10 minutes, or until the straws puff and are golden. Repeat with the remaining pastry. Serve the straws warm or at room temperature. Store the straws in an airtight container, where they will keep for 2 to 3 days.

Makes 18 straws

In 1305, anise seed was taxed to help pay for repairs to London Bridge.

Spice-Crusted Cheese Truffles

Cheese goes well with herbs and spices. Here are several variations of a basic cheese truffle, bite-size treats your guests will love.

½ cup shredded cheddar cheese
4 ounces cream cheese, at room temperature
2 teaspoons finely minced white or yellow onion
½ teaspoon Worcestershire sauce
¼ teaspoon black pepper
5 teaspoons ground mild chile pepper

Cream together the cheddar cheese, cream cheese, onion, Worcestershire, and pepper in a medium mixing bowl until light and fluffy. Cover and refrigerate for 1 hour.

Roll the cheese into 1-inch-round balls. Roll each truffle in the chile pepper. Serve immediately or refrigerate until ready to use.

Makes 18 (1-inch) truffles

Variations: Substitute the following cheeses (for the cheddar) and spice (for the chile pepper) to create tasty Spice-Crusted Cheese Truffle variations:
- *½ cup shredded Havarti cheese and 5 teaspoons dill weed*
- *¼ cup crumbled feta cheese and 5 teaspoons oregano*
- *¼ cup crumbled blue cheese and 5 teaspoons dried orange zest*
- *¼ cup crumbled chèvre cheese and 5 teaspoons basil*

Hard-Boiled Eggs

Bring 3 quarts of water to a boil in a medium saucepan. Gently lower the eggs into the water with a slotted spoon. Allow the water to return to a boil and then immediately decrease the heat and simmer the eggs for 14 minutes. Using a slotted spoon, remove the eggs from the boiling water and place them into a bowl of ice water to prevent further cooking. Let stand until the eggs are cool enough to handle, then peel the eggs.

Deviled Eggs

There are two schools of thought on deviled eggs—mayonnaise or sour cream. We have always been firmly in the mayo camp, but we've been convinced that the sour cream approach has some advantages as well. Sour cream and mayonnaise are easily substituted for each other in the following recipes. And since deviled eggs are easy and popular appetizers, we've included two of our favorite versions. Feel free to try other herb or spice combinations. The rule for deviled eggs, as for so many foods, is simple: suit yourself!

Dilled Deviled Eggs

8 hard-boiled eggs (see page 76)
6 tablespoons sour cream
1 tablespoon Dijon mustard
2 teaspoons minced shallots
2 teaspoons dill weed
½ teaspoon vinegar
Salt
Freshly cracked pepper, for garnish (optional)

Slice each egg in half lengthwise. Scoop the yolks into a small bowl and set the whites aside. Add the sour cream, mustard, shallots, dill weed, and vinegar to the egg yolks and, using a fork, stir to thoroughly combine. Season the egg mixture with salt to taste. Place the mixture into a small plastic sandwich zipper bag, close the zipper, and cut a small hole at one of the corners. Arrange the egg whites cut side up on a serving plate. Pipe the mixture into each of the egg white halves. Garnish the top of each deviled egg with pepper, if using. Chill the eggs in the refrigerator for at least 1 hour before serving.

Makes 16 deviled eggs

Curried Deviled Eggs

. . . .

8 hard-boiled eggs (see page 76)
6 tablespoons mayonnaise
3 teaspoons Dijon mustard
2 teaspoons minced shallots
2 teaspoons ground cumin
2 teaspoons ground coriander
1 teaspoon ground turmeric
½ teaspoon vinegar
Salt
Freshly cracked pepper, for garnish (optional)

Slice each egg in half lengthwise. Scoop the yolks into a small bowl and set the whites aside. Add the mayonnaise, mustard, shallots, cumin, coriander, turmeric, and vinegar to the egg yolks and, using a fork, stir to thoroughly combine. Season the egg mixture with salt to taste. Place the mixture into a small plastic sandwich bag and cut a small hole at one of the corners. Arrange the egg whites cut side up on a serving plate. Pipe the mixture into each of the egg white halves. Garnish the top of each deviled egg with freshly cracked pepper, if using. Chill the eggs in the refrigerator for at least 1 hour before serving.

Makes 16 deviled eggs

Variation: For a touch of heat, add 1 teaspoon ground mild chile pepper.

Cardamom Candied Walnuts

Careful, these nuts are addictive. They're delicious all by themselves, and they play a starring role in some other recipes in this book—Chicken Salad (page 65), Waldorf Salad (page 53), and our Caramel Apple Sundaes (page 182). That's a good reason to make a double batch.

1 egg white
¼ cup sugar
1 teaspoon ground cinnamon
1 teaspoon ground green cardamom
2½ cups walnut halves

Preheat the oven to 350°F. Whisk together the egg white, sugar, cinnamon, and cardamom in a small bowl. Pour the egg mixture into a large resealable plastic bag. Add the walnuts, seal the bag, and shake until the walnuts are evenly coated.

Grease a jelly roll pan. Spread the walnuts in a single layer and bake for 10 minutes, stirring halfway through baking. Remove the pan from the oven, loosen the walnuts, and let cool for 10 minutes. Store the walnuts in an airtight container.

Makes 2½ cups

fun fact

Cardamom, often called the Queen of Spices, belongs to the ginger family and is native to India and Sri Lanka.

Herb-Stuffed Mushrooms

Stuffed mushrooms are an easy sell at any party. Seasoned with aromatic organic herbs, they are even more alluring. With walnuts, Parmesan, and cream cheese, this recipe comes pretty close to an all-time party favorite.

4 ounces plus 12 ounces mushrooms
⅓ cup (⅔ stick) butter
⅓ cup finely diced onion (any variety)
2 scallions, finely chopped
1 rib of celery, finely diced
1 clove garlic, minced
⅔ cup finely chopped walnuts
1 teaspoon basil

1 teaspoon thyme
1 teaspoon oregano
½ teaspoon rosemary
¼ teaspoon salt
¼ teaspoon black pepper
4 ounces cream cheese, cut into cubes and softened
2 tablespoons freshly grated Parmesan cheese

Preheat the oven to 375°F. Finely chop 4 ounces of the mushrooms, including stems, and set aside. Melt the butter in a large saucepan over medium heat. Add the onion, scallions, and celery to the pan and sauté until tender, about 4 minutes. Add the garlic and cook, stirring continually, for 1 minute. Add the chopped mushrooms and walnuts and cook, stirring continually, for 3 minutes. Stir in the basil, thyme, oregano, rosemary, salt, and pepper and continue cooking for 3 minutes. Add the cream cheese and stir until the mushroom filling and cream cheese are thoroughly combined.

Remove and discard the stems from the remaining 12 ounces of mushrooms. Arrange the mushroom caps, stem side up, in a 13 by 9 by 2-inch baking dish. Fill each mushroom with a heaping teaspoon of the mushroom filling. Sprinkle ¼ teaspoon of Parmesan cheese on top of each mushroom cap. Bake until the mushroom tops are bubbling, about 15 minutes. Serve the stuffed mushrooms warm.

Makes 24 mushrooms

Basil is a member of the mint family. It has been cultivated in the warmer parts of Asia for at least 3,000 years.

Tangy Tarragon Deviled Potatoes

These deviled potatoes make great appetizers. Select potatoes that are similar in shape and size to a large egg.

14 small red potatoes
1 tablespoon olive oil
1 teaspoon kosher salt
¼ cup sour cream
2 teaspoons fresh lemon juice
2 teaspoons minced shallots
1 teaspoon Dijon mustard
1 teaspoon sugar
1 teaspoon tarragon
¼ teaspoon coarse black pepper,
    plus extra for garnish
Salt

Preheat the oven to 350°F. Place the potatoes in a medium bowl. Drizzle the olive oil over the potatoes and toss the potatoes until thoroughly coated. Sprinkle 1 teaspoon of kosher salt over the potatoes and gently toss to coat. Place the potatoes onto a large baking sheet. Bake the potatoes until tender, 40 to 45 minutes. Remove the potatoes from the oven and let cool for 15 minutes.

Slice each potato in half lengthwise. Using a ½ teaspoon measuring spoon, scoop out the center from each potato half, leaving the shell intact, and place it in a medium bowl. Discard 4 of the potato skin shells and set the remaining shells aside. Add the sour cream, lemon juice, shallots, mustard, sugar, tarragon, and ¼ teaspoon of pepper to the bowl of potatoes and, using a potato masher, mash until thoroughly combined. Season the potato mixture with salt to taste.

Arrange the potato skin shells cut side up on a serving plate. Spoon the potato mixture into each of the potato shells. Garnish the top of each deviled potato with coarse black pepper. Serve the deviled potatoes at room temperature.

Makes 24 deviled potatoes

fun fact

French tarragon does not flower, so the plant has been painstakingly cultivated from cuttings and roots for hundreds of years. Thomas Jefferson was an early enthusiast and propagated the plant in the U.S., perhaps having learned of it on his visits to France.

Spicy Middle Eastern Chicken Skewers

This medley of spice flavors brings out the best in chicken. These skewers are great for hors d'oeuvres, but they're so good there will be times you will want to reserve them for the main course.

1½ pounds chicken tenders
2 tablespoons olive oil
2 teaspoons ground ancho chile pepper **or**
    mild chile pepper
2 teaspoons ground cinnamon
2 teaspoons ground coriander
2 teaspoons ground cumin
2 teaspoons ground turmeric
2 teaspoons dry mustard powder
1½ teaspoons coarse salt
½ cup Lemon Dill Aïoli (recipe follows)

Preheat the grill to medium. Soak bamboo skewers (one for each chicken tender) in a shallow dish of water. Place the chicken in a large resealable plastic bag. Add the oil, seal the bag, and shake until the chicken is thoroughly coated with the oil. Combine the ancho chile pepper, cinnamon, coriander, cumin, turmeric, mustard powder, and salt in a small bowl. Add the seasoning mixture to the chicken, seal the bag, and gently knead the chicken, working the seasoning in so that it evenly coats the chicken. Carefully thread each chicken tender onto a skewer.

Grill the chicken skewers, turning once, until the internal temperature reaches 165°F, 3 to 4 minutes per side. Serve immediately with aïoli for dipping.

Makes 4 main or 6 to 8 appetizer servings

fun fact

In *A Thousand and One Nights*, the clever Scheherazade avoids execution by regaling her cruel husband with a story each night, until he falls so deeply in love that he finally spares her life. But could it have been the coriander? In her tales, Scheherazade mentions its aphrodisiac powers.

Lemon Dill Aïoli

. . . .

This spread is delicious on sandwiches and in chicken or turkey salad. You can also vary the flavor by substituting a different herb or spice for the dill, such as oregano or basil, cumin or coriander.

½ cup mayonnaise
2 cloves garlic, minced
1 teaspoon dill weed
1 teaspoon dried lemon zest
½ teaspoon lemon juice
¼ teaspoon salt

Whisk together the mayonnaise, garlic, dill weed, lemon zest, lemon juice, and salt in a small bowl. Serve immediately or cover and store in the refrigerator for up to 1 week.

Makes ½ cup

Medieval German brides and grooms carried dill, salt, and cumin in their pockets during the wedding ceremony to ensure that they would remain faithful to each other.

Spiced Guacamole

A good, ripe avocado really doesn't need much help to become a delicious homemade guacamole. Serve it with chips and be prepared for it to disappear quickly.

3 medium ripe avocados
1 teaspoon ground mild chile pepper
¾ teaspoon lime juice
½ teaspoon garlic salt

Cut the avocados in half and remove the pits. Scoop out the avocado from the peel and put it in a medium mixing bowl. Mash the avocados. Stir in the mild chile pepper, lime juice, and garlic salt. Serve the guacamole immediately.

Makes approximately 1½ cups

fun fact

Although they have been cultivated for more than 5,000 years, chile peppers were unknown outside of the Americas before 1492. Spanish and Portuguese traders introduced them to Europe and Asia. Today, one-fifth of the world's people eat chile pepper. It is used in cuisines around the world, including Indian, Thai, Chinese, and Hungarian. And, of course, chile peppers remain a favorite in many parts of the Americas.

Cumin-Cilantro Sour Cream Dip

This tangy dip is perfect for veggies, chips, or baked potato skins.

**1 cup sour cream or whole plain yogurt,
    preferably Greek style
1 tablespoon chopped cilantro
1 teaspoon ground cumin
½ teaspoon fresh lime juice
½ teaspoon garlic powder
Salt**

Whisk together the sour cream, cilantro, cumin, lime juice, and garlic powder in a small bowl. Season the dip with salt to taste, about ½ teaspoon. Serve immediately or cover and chill before serving.

Makes 1 cup

Cumin, beloved by the ancient Roman cookbook author Apicius, was heralded for its ability to cure gas. This earthy spice is generally considered good for digestion, and in northern India, "cumin coolers" are a popular summer drink.

Creole-Spiced Popcorn

Popcorn needs to be crisp, and the trouble with butter is that it turns the kernels soggy. We've solved that by spreading the seasoned popcorn on a jelly roll pan and baking just long enough to crisp the kernels. That way, you can have crunchy popcorn and buttered seasoning too.

15 cups popped popcorn
4 tablespoons (½ stick) unsalted butter, melted
1 tablespoon Creole Seasoning (recipe follows)

Preheat the oven to 300°F. Remove all of the unpopped kernels from the popped corn. Place the popped corn into a large mixing bowl. Combine the butter and Creole seasoning in a small bowl. Pour the seasoned butter over the popped corn and gently toss, using two forks, until the popcorn is evenly coated.

Spread the popcorn in a single layer on a jelly roll pan. Bake the popcorn for 5 minutes, or until the popcorn has reached the desired crispness. Serve immediately or store in an airtight container for up to 1 week.

Makes 15 cups

Creole Seasoning

This versatile seasoning is also good sprinkled on fish, chicken, pork, shrimp, vegetables, or potatoes.

2 teaspoons garlic powder
2 teaspoons kosher salt
1 teaspoon ground ancho chile pepper
1 teaspoon oregano
1 teaspoon thyme
1 teaspoon onion powder
1 teaspoon black pepper

Combine all the ingredients for the seasoning in a small bowl. Store any unused seasoning in an airtight container.

fun fact

While most of the world's chile peppers are now grown in Asia, ancho chile pepper, the dried form of the poblano chile, is cultivated only in the Americas.

Clove-Spiced Caramel Corn

Here's a snack to love—fresh, homemade caramel corn. The cloves lend a wonderful flavor and aroma to this popular treat.

12 cups popped popcorn
8 tablespoons (1 stick) butter
⅔ cup firmly packed brown sugar
2 tablespoons maple syrup
1 teaspoon ground cloves
½ teaspoon vanilla
⅛ teaspoon salt
¼ teaspoon baking soda

Preheat the oven to 300°F. Remove all of the unpopped kernels from the popped corn. Place the popcorn into a large mixing bowl. Combine the butter, brown sugar, maple syrup, cloves, vanilla, and salt in a medium saucepan. Cook the caramel mixture over medium heat, stirring continually, until the sugar has dissolved. Allow the mixture to come to a boil and continue boiling the caramel, over medium heat, without stirring, for 5 minutes. Remove the saucepan from the heat and stir in the baking soda. Pour the caramel over the popcorn and gently toss, using two forks, until the popcorn is evenly coated with caramel.

Spread the caramel corn in a single layer on a jelly roll pan. Bake the caramel corn for 15 minutes, stirring every 5 minutes. Remove the caramel corn from the oven and allow to cool before serving. Store the caramel corn in an airtight container for up to 1 week.

Makes 12 cups

"No merchants or sailors . . . have ever seen the kind of tree that produces cloves: its fruit, they say, is sold by genies . . . ," wrote Ibrahim ibn Wasif-Shah in the tenth century. He reported that merchants obtained cloves by setting goods ashore and retreating to their ships; during the night, genies replaced them with the sought-after spice.

Entrées

The dinner table is the heart of a home, the place where family members and guests gather for sustenance—and not just the sustenance of food. Dinnertime is also the time for family members to talk, to catch up on the day's activities, to tell stories, to laugh, to debate, and, of course, to eat.

When all is said and done, the dinner table may do more to bond us to one another than almost any other part of our daily routine. No wonder studies show that the more often children and adolescents participate in family dinners, the lower their chances of dabbling in risky behaviors and the higher their chances of success in school. We love spending time around the dinner table, and we firmly believe that good food is a catalyst for lively conversation and for the good times that shore up our bonds to family members and friends, old and new.

This chapter features dishes that are full of flavor without requiring enormous expenditures of time and effort. They are suitable for family meals and for dinner parties. Whether it's an easy and sensational mac and cheese (a perfect vegetarian meal), jazzed-up burgers, or appealing ways to vary the ubiquitous chicken, this chapter offers you a variety of ideas for spicing up your favorite foods. Some of them offer new flavor combinations or updates of familiar foods. All of them are worth lingering over at the dinner table.

Chili Powder

This is a nicely balanced chili powder mixture, but feel free to tweak it to your own personal chili preferences.

1 tablespoon ground cumin
2 teaspoons ground ancho chile pepper
2 teaspoons ground mild chile pepper
2 teaspoons oregano
1 teaspoon fennel seed

Combine all the ingredients and mix well. Store the mixture in an airtight container in a cool, dark place for up to 2 months.

Makes 10 teaspoons

Game Day Chili

● ●

We call this Game Day Chili because it's perfect for all those fall and winter ball games. But don't limit it to sports occasions. This is a chili you'll want to make—and enjoy—over and over again.

2 pounds lean ground beef
1½ cups chopped onion (any variety)
1 recipe Chili Powder (page 95)
2 (15-ounce) cans red beans, drained and rinsed
4 cups tomato juice
1 (29-ounce) can tomato sauce
1½ teaspoons garlic powder
1 teaspoon salt
½ teaspoon black pepper
Shredded cheese, for topping (optional)
Chopped green onions, for topping (optional)

Brown the ground beef and onion in a large saucepot or Dutch oven over medium-high heat; drain the fat. Stir in the chili powder and cook for 2 minutes. Stir in the red beans, tomato juice, tomato sauce, garlic powder, salt, and pepper. Bring to a boil, decrease the heat to low, and simmer for 30 minutes, stirring occasionally. Serve the chili topped with cheese and green onions, if using.

Southwestern Chicken Chili

Lighter than beef chili but every bit as flavorful, this chicken-based version features the flavors of the Southwest without overpowering your palate. This recipe is perfect for family suppers any time of the year.

1 tablespoon olive oil
1½ cups diced onion (any variety)
1½ cups diced tomatillos
4 cloves garlic, minced
2 cups diced fresh tomatoes
2 cups cooked shredded chicken
1 tablespoon ground cumin
1 teaspoon ground ancho chile pepper
    or mild chile pepper
3 cups chicken broth
2 (15-ounce) cans navy beans, undrained
¼ cup chopped cilantro, plus additional for topping
1 tablespoon fresh lime juice (optional)
Salt and black pepper
Shredded Monterey Jack cheese, for topping
Sour cream, for topping

Heat the oil in a large saucepan over medium-high heat. Add the onion and sauté for 3 minutes. Add the tomatillos and sauté for an additional 3 minutes. Add the garlic and tomatoes and cook, stirring occasionally, for 5 minutes. Stir in the chicken, cumin, and ancho chile. Add the chicken broth and beans and cook until the soup is heated through. Stir in the cilantro and lime juice, if using, and season the soup with salt and pepper to taste. Serve the soup topped with cheese, sour cream, and additional cilantro.

Makes 8 cups

Macaroni and Cheese

Ever since we discovered a version of mac and cheese that didn't require boiling the pasta first, we've been devotees of this beloved American comfort food. It's perfect for kids and crowds and has become a potluck favorite, where vegetarians are grateful for nonmeat entrées.

If you get a hint of pepperoni in this version, you're not wrong—anise and basil are the flavors that give that popular sausage its distinctive flavor. As always, feel free to come up with your own spice combinations. We like substituting fennel seed for the anise seed and tarragon for the basil.

1 cup cottage cheese (not low fat)
2 cups milk (not skim)
1 teaspoon ground mild chile pepper
1 teaspoon anise seed
1 teaspoon dry mustard powder
½ teaspoon salt
¼ teaspoon black pepper
8 ounces extra sharp
    cheddar cheese, grated

8 ounces Monterey Jack cheese, grated
½ pound elbow pasta, uncooked
¼ cup plain breadcrumbs
¼ cup freshly grated Parmesan
    cheese
1 teaspoon basil
1 tablespoon olive oil

Preheat the oven to 375°F. Blend the cottage cheese, milk, chile pepper, anise seed, mustard, salt, and pepper in a blender until smooth. Pour the mixture into a large mixing bowl. Stir in the cheddar cheese, Monterey Jack cheese, and pasta. Grease an 8-inch square or round baking dish. Pour the pasta mixture into the dish. Cover the pan tightly with aluminum foil and bake for 40 minutes.

While the macaroni and cheese is baking, mix the breadcrumbs, Parmesan cheese, and basil in a small bowl. Add the oil and toss to combine. Remove the macaroni and cheese from the oven and carefully stir. Evenly sprinkle the breadcrumbs on top of the macaroni and cheese. Return the macaroni and cheese to the oven and bake, uncovered, for 10 minutes, or until browned. Let cool for 10 minutes before serving.

Serves 6 to 8

Variations:
- *Substitute fennel seed for the anise seed and tarragon for the basil.*
- *Add a teaspoon of mild chile pepper and omit the breadcrumb topping.*

Grilled Cheddar Burgers

A good burger is a glorious thing, a simple but oh-so-satisfying meal. Burgers love to be dressed up and not just with condiments. Sneak some spices, seasonings, and cheese into the meat, and you have a yummy burger indeed.

1 pound ground beef
½ cup shredded cheddar cheese
2 teaspoons ground ancho chile pepper
   or mild chile pepper
1 teaspoon dried lemon zest
1 teaspoon garlic powder
1 teaspoon onion powder
4 hamburger buns
Favorite burger toppings (lettuce, tomatoes, onions, pickles, ketchup, mustard, mayonnaise, etc.)

Preheat the grill to medium-high. Mix the ground beef, cheese, ancho chile, lemon zest, garlic powder, and onion powder together in a medium bowl. Divide the meat into 4 equal portions and form each into a burger patty that is 1 inch thick. Grill the burgers, flipping once, to the desired doneness. Place the burger patties on the hamburger buns, add your favorite burger toppings, and serve.

Serves 4

fun fact

Chile peppers' hotness is measured in Scoville Heat Units (SHU). The measurement is named after the pharmacist Wilbur Scoville, who invented the system in 1912. Sweet bell peppers score 0, jalapeño peppers 3,000–6,000, and habañero peppers a flame-throwing 500,000. Generally, the smaller the pepper, the hotter it will be.

Hamburger Stroganoff

• •

This is one of Sara's favorite weeknight dinners. It's quick and easy—and there's never a problem with leftovers. This recipe also works well with ground turkey.

1 pound lean ground beef
4 tablespoons (½ stick) butter
¾ cup diced onion (any variety)
1 clove garlic, minced
8 ounces sliced mushrooms
2 teaspoons marjoram
¼ cup all-purpose flour
1¾ cups beef broth
1 cup sour cream
Salt and black pepper
Cooked egg noodles, rice, or pasta, for serving

Brown the ground beef in a large skillet over medium-high heat until crumbly. Remove the ground beef from the pan and cover to keep warm. In the same skillet, melt the butter over medium heat. Add the onion to the pan and sauté until tender, about 5 minutes. Add the garlic and the mushrooms and cook, stirring occasionally, until the mushrooms are tender, about 5 minutes. Add the marjoram and flour and cook, stirring constantly, for 2 minutes. Return the ground beef to the pan and stir to combine. Whisk in the beef broth and cook, stirring occasionally, until the sauce begins to thicken, about 5 minutes. Decrease the heat to low, stir in the sour cream, and cook until heated through. Season the stroganoff with salt and pepper to taste and serve over egg noodles, rice, or pasta.

Serves 4 to 6

Variation: Substitute 1 pound ground turkey for the beef.

Marjoram is often called "knotted marjoram" because its delicate pastel flowers bloom from tiny, knotlike green buds along its stem.

Spice-Rubbed Baby Back Ribs

These ribs are simple to make and addictive to eat. The rub was devised by Katie's daughter, Diana, one of the most spice-enlightened young ladies we know—and already a great cook. Diana explored widely in the spice cabinet to come up with this rub, and we think you'll agree that the results are spectacular.

These ribs are so good, Sara has successfully used the promise of a rib dinner to extract yard work from teenage boys. The ribs are also fabulous grilled or smoked on a barbecue (note the cooking time below).

⅔ cup Rib Rub (recipe follows)
2 (2 pounds each) racks baby back ribs

Spread ⅓ cup of the rub all over each rack of ribs. Cover the ribs with aluminum foil and refrigerate for at least 2 hours or up to 8 hours.

Preheat the oven to 350°F. Remove the ribs from the refrigerator and place on a baking sheet. Bake the ribs for 60 minutes, or until tender. Unwrap the foil and bake the ribs for an additional 15 to 30 minutes, or until the ribs are browned.

These ribs can also be cooked on a very slow grill for 1½ to 2 hours, turning once after 45 minutes and checking frequently after 1½ hours.

Serves 8

Rib Rub

Smoked pimentón, or smoked paprika, is a Spanish specialty that is gradually becoming easier to find in this country. It's worth asking for at a specialty food store, but if it's not available, substitute regular paprika, either hot or sweet.

¼ cup firmly packed brown sugar
1 tablespoon sea salt
1 tablespoon hot or sweet pimentón or hot or sweet paprika
2 teaspoons onion powder
2 teaspoons garlic powder
2 teaspoons dried lemon zest
2 teaspoons ground ancho chile pepper
2 teaspoons ground cumin
1 teaspoon thyme
1 teaspoon oregano
1 teaspoon ground coriander
1 teaspoon fennel seed

Combine all the ingredients in a small mixing bowl. Use the rub immediately or store in an airtight container in a cool, dark place for up to 2 months.

Makes approximately ⅔ cup

fun fact

The name of "Marathon," where the Greeks of Athens defeated the Persians in 490, is said to refer to the abundant wild fennel that covered its plain.

Chile, Orange, and Coriander–Rubbed Pork

 with

Balsamic Glaze

• •

Chile pepper, orange zest, and coriander are the perfect trio to dress up pork tenderloin. This dish is easy to prepare and works equally well for a family meal (the leftover pork makes a great lunch sandwich) or for dinner parties. The pork medallions make such a beautiful presentation that you'll have a hard time convincing everybody you weren't in the kitchen all day long.

> **2 tablespoons olive oil**
> **2 teaspoons ground ancho chile pepper or mild chile**
>   **pepper**
> **2 teaspoons ground coriander**
> **2 teaspoons dried orange zest**
> **1 teaspoon coarse salt**
> **2 (1 to 1½ pounds each) pork tenderloins**
> **⅔ cup balsamic vinegar**
> **⅓ cup orange juice**

Preheat the oven to 350°F. Combine the oil, ancho chile, coriander, orange zest, and salt in a small bowl. Spread the rub evenly over all sides of the pork tenderloins and rub into the meat. Bake the pork tenderloin in an oven/stovetop-safe pan until the internal temperature reaches 155°F, 40 to 50 minutes. Remove the pork from the pan and let stand for 10 minutes.

While the meat is resting, warm the remaining pan drippings on the stove over medium-high heat. Pour in the vinegar to deglaze the pan. While stirring continually, add the orange juice and reduce the liquid until it thickens and forms a glaze that coats the back of a spoon, about 5 minutes.

Slice the pork tenderloin into ¾-inch-wide medallions. Arrange the sliced pork on a platter and drizzle with balsamic glaze.

Serves 4 to 6

Coriander lends a fresh scent to perfumes, incense, and cosmetics. The pharmaceutical industry uses its essential oil in migraine remedies and to soothe indigestion.

Grilled Pork Chops with Cumin-Lime Butter

It's hard to go wrong with grilled pork chops, but the well-matched trio of cumin, chile pepper, and oregano shows how a well-seasoned imagination can give a familiar favorite a new dimension. Top each pork chop with Cumin-Lime Butter. Feel free to substitute mild chile pepper for the ancho.

1 teaspoon ground cumin
1 teaspoon ground ancho chile pepper
1 teaspoon oregano
1 teaspoon coarse salt
4 (½-inch-thick) boneless pork loin chops
¼ cup Cumin-Lime Butter (recipe follows)

Preheat the grill to medium. Combine the cumin, ancho chile, oregano, and salt in a small bowl. Sprinkle the seasoning mixture evenly over both sides of each pork chop, ½ teaspoon of seasoning per side, and press into the meat. Grill the pork chops, turning once, until the internal temperature reaches 155°F, about 6 minutes per side. Serve each pork chop topped with 1 tablespoon of cumin-lime butter.

Serves 4

Cumin-Lime Butter

Infused with the earthy warmth of cumin and the zesty brightness of lime, this butter knows how to dress up a pork chop. You'll find plenty of other uses for it as well, from grilled chicken to corn on the cob.

4 tablespoons (½ stick) unsalted butter, at room temperature
1½ teaspoons freshly squeezed lime juice
1 teaspoon ground cumin
Salt

Combine the butter, lime juice, and cumin in a small bowl. Stir in the salt to taste. Serve the butter immediately. Store leftover butter in an airtight container in the refrigerator.

Makes ¼ cup

fun fact

In medieval Europe, cumin was thought to bring back lost or stolen objects and to keep lovers and livestock from straying. Women gave departing Crusaders cumin-flavored wine or loaves of cumin bread to ensure their safe return.

Tarragon Chicken Potpie

If you're lucky enough to know (or remember) how good a homemade chicken potpie can be, here's your chance to create (or revisit) some fabulous food memories. Tarragon is sweetly assertive and works especially well with chicken.

4 tablespoons (½ stick) butter
2 cups diced onion (any variety)
¼ cup chopped celery
⅓ cup all-purpose flour
1 teaspoon tarragon
½ teaspoon salt
¼ teaspoon black pepper
2 cups chicken broth
1 cup heavy cream or half-and-half
2 cups diced cooked chicken
1 cup diced cooked potatoes
1 cup diced cooked carrots
1 cup peas, fresh or frozen and thawed
Basic Pie Crust Dough (page 169),
**   made with coriander**

Preheat the oven to 375°F. Melt the butter over medium heat in a large skillet. Stir in the onion and celery and sauté until tender, about 5 minutes. Add the flour, tarragon, salt, and pepper and stir to combine. Pour in the chicken broth and cook, stirring continually, for 5 minutes. Stir in the cream and cook, stirring often, for an additional 10 minutes. Add the chicken, potatoes, carrots, and peas to the sauce and stir to combine. Pour the chicken mixture into a 1½-quart casserole dish. Place the pie crust dough on top of the casserole dish. Moisten the rim of the casserole dish to help the pastry adhere, and fold the edges of the dough under, sealing the dough to the casserole dish. Cut vents in the crust to allow for steam to escape and bake the potpie for 40 minutes, or until the crust is golden.

Serves 4 to 6

fun fact

Tarragon's Latin name, *Artemisia dracunculus*, alludes to a "little dragon," perhaps because chewing the raw plant can numb the tip of the tongue. This may be what a 1538 English text means when it claims tarragon "hath a tast like gynger [sic]."

Fruit Juice–Glazed Barbecued Chicken

It's easy to buy a bottle of barbecue sauce, but once you try this sweet and spicy version, you won't want to go commercial again—and your kids won't let you. This is a great family dinner and equally good for a grilled dinner with friends. If you have any left over, save it for later. The chicken is just as good cold as hot off the grill.

½ **cup pineapple juice**
½ **cup freshly squeezed lime juice**
½ **cup firmly packed brown sugar**
¼ **cup ketchup**
¼ **cup soy sauce**
2 **tablespoons plus 1 tablespoon vegetable oil**
2 **tablespoons minced garlic**
2 **teaspoons ground mild chile pepper**
2 **teaspoons dried lemon zest**
2 **teaspoons ground ginger**
8 **bone-in, skin-on chicken thighs or drumsticks**
Salt and coarse black pepper

Preheat the grill to medium. Whisk together the pineapple juice, lime juice, brown sugar, ketchup, soy sauce, 2 tablespoons of the oil, garlic, chile pepper, lemon zest, and ginger in a small saucepan. Bring the fruit juice glaze to a boil over high heat and cook, stirring often, until the glaze thickens and is reduced by half, about 8 minutes.

While the glaze is reducing, brush the chicken with the remaining 1 tablespoon of oil and season with salt and pepper. Grill the chicken until it is thoroughly cooked and the internal temperature reaches 165°F. Generously brush the chicken with the fruit juice glaze the last 5 minutes of grilling.

Serves 4

Black pepper and ginger were the two most commonly traded spices in the thirteenth and fourteenth centuries.

Parmesan Chicken

• •

This recipe sounds rich—and it is. But there's just enough sauce to remind you of what comfort food is all about. The basil gently complements the chicken, cheese, and cream, while the artichoke hearts add the right amount of texture. If you just can't spend all those calories on whipping cream, don't despair. This dish is good with low-fat cream.

6 tablespoons plus 2 tablespoons unsalted butter
1½ pounds chicken tenders
1½ cups freshly grated Parmesan cheese
½ cup whipping cream
2 teaspoons basil
2 cloves garlic, minced
½ teaspoon black pepper
1 (14-ounce) can quartered artichoke hearts,
  well drained

Melt 2 tablespoons of the butter in a large skillet over medium heat. Add the chicken and sauté until cooked through and browned. Remove from the heat and keep warm.

Melt the remaining 6 tablespoons of butter in a large skillet over low heat. Add the cheese, whipping cream, basil, garlic, and pepper and stir continually until the cheese is melted. Add the artichokes and cook over low heat until heated through.

Place the cooked chicken in a serving dish and pour the sauce evenly over the chicken. Serve immediately.

Serves 4

Variations:
- *Substitute tarragon or another herb for the basil.*
- *For a different flavor profile, omit the basil and use 1 teaspoon of cumin and 1 teaspoon of coriander. If you like, add 1 teaspoon of turmeric. This will give the dish an earthy depth of flavor and a brightly colored hue.*
- *If you'd like a touch of heat, omit the basil and use 1 teaspoon of coriander and 1 teaspoon of mild chile pepper.*

Chicken Fajitas

• •

Fajitas are a family favorite. But a lot of seasoning blends contain more salt and additives than flavor. This tasty version shows how easy it is to spice your own and how much better the fajitas taste with pure, organic herbs and spices.

¼ cup lime juice
2 tablespoons plus 2 tablespoons vegetable oil
2 teaspoons ground ancho chile pepper
2 teaspoons ground cumin
2 teaspoons oregano
2 teaspoons garlic powder
2 teaspoons seasoned salt
1 pound boneless, skinless chicken breasts,
**   cut into thin strips**
1 medium red bell pepper, cut into thin strips
1 medium green bell pepper, cut into thin strips
1 medium onion (any variety), halved and thinly sliced
8 (8-inch) flour tortillas, warmed
Spiced Guacamole (page 85), for topping
Cumin-Cilantro Sour Cream Dip (page 87), for topping
Shredded cheddar cheese, for topping

Combine the lime juice, 2 tablespoons of the oil, ancho chile, cumin, oregano, garlic powder, and seasoned salt in a medium bowl. Add the chicken to the marinade, cover, and refrigerate for 1 hour.

Heat the remaining 2 tablespoons of oil in a large skillet over medium-high heat. Add the bell peppers and onion and sauté until crisp-tender, about 4 minutes. Remove the peppers and onion from the skillet and keep warm. In the same skillet, add the chicken along with the marinade and cook over medium-high heat, stirring continually, until the chicken is thoroughly cooked, 5 to 6 minutes. Return the peppers and onion to the pan and cook until heated through. To serve, spoon the chicken fajita filling onto the tortillas and top with the guacamole, sour cream, and cheese.

Makes 8 fajitas

Herb-Crusted Chicken

. . . .

This crusted chicken is easy to prepare and full of flavor, two outstanding reasons to add it to your repertoire of favorite recipes. It can be the main dish for dinner, or you can cut it in strips to top off a satisfying luncheon salad.

⅓ cup plain breadcrumbs
¼ cup freshly grated Parmesan cheese
2 teaspoons basil
1 teaspoon oregano
1 teaspoon dry mustard
1 teaspoon garlic powder
½ teaspoon salt
2 tablespoons olive oil
2 tablespoons butter, melted
4 boneless, skinless chicken breasts

Preheat the oven to 350°F. Grease a baking sheet or spray with nonstick cooking spray. Combine the breadcrumbs, cheese, basil, oregano, mustard, garlic powder, and salt in a wide, shallow dish. In another wide, shallow dish, combine the oil and butter. Dip the chicken, one piece at a time, into the oil and butter mixture and then thoroughly coat with the breadcrumb mixture. Place the coated chicken breasts onto the baking sheet. Bake the chicken until it is golden brown and the internal temperature reaches 165°F, about 45 minutes.

Serves 4

Variation: Substitute 1 teaspoon of ground mild chile pepper and 1 teaspoon of ground cumin for the basil and oregano.

fun fact

In Romania, if a boy accepts a sprig of basil from a girl, it means he returns her affection, while girls in Moldavia tame wandering ways by secretly slipping sprigs of basil into their boyfriends' pockets or clothing.

Chicken Enchilada Casserole

This cheesy casserole embodies all our favorite things about comfort food—well seasoned, but full of the down-home goodness of basic ingredients. This is a perfect casserole for a one-dish weeknight supper, a great backdrop for family conversation after a busy day at school and work.

1 tablespoon canola or other mild-tasting oil	½ cup all-purpose flour
1½ cups diced onion (any variety)	1¼ cups chicken stock
1 clove garlic, minced	1¼ cups whole milk
1 teaspoon ground coriander	1 (10-ounce) can diced tomatoes and green chiles
1 teaspoon oregano	1 cup grated Monterey Jack cheese
1 teaspoon ground cumin	1 cup plus 1½ cups grated cheddar cheese, plus additional for topping
1 teaspoon ground ancho chile pepper	Salt and black pepper
2 cups diced cooked chicken	10 (6-inch) corn tortillas
8 tablespoons (1 stick) butter	

Preheat the oven to 350°F. Heat the oil in a medium skillet over medium heat. Add the onion to the pan and sauté until tender, about 5 minutes. Add the garlic, coriander, oregano, cumin, and ancho chile pepper and cook, stirring continually, for 1 minute. Remove ½ cup of the onion mixture from the pan and set aside. Decrease the heat to low, add the chicken to the skillet, and cook, stirring occasionally, until heated through.

While the chicken is heating, melt the butter in a medium saucepan over medium heat. Whisk in the flour and cook, stirring constantly, for 3 minutes. Whisk in the chicken stock and milk and cook, stirring often, for 5 minutes. Add the diced tomatoes and green chiles and the ½ cup onion mixture, and cook, stirring often, for 5 minutes. Remove the saucepan from the heat. Add the Monterey Jack and 1 cup of the cheddar cheese and stir until the cheese melts. Season the sauce with salt and pepper to taste.

Place 1 cup of the sauce in the bottom of a 13 by 9 by 2-inch baking dish. Dip each tortilla in the remaining sauce. Place ¼ cup of the hot chicken and onions, and 2 tablespoons of the cheddar cheese, in the center of each coated tortilla and roll up. Place the enchiladas seam side down in the baking dish. Top with the remaining sauce and bake, uncovered, for 15 minutes. Remove the enchilada casserole from the oven and top immediately with additional cheddar cheese.

Serves 6

Jamaican Jerk Chicken

All the best flavors of the Caribbean come together in this marinade. You'll be amazed at what they can do for chicken on the grill. And you'll see what people mean when they talk about a spice party for your palate. Feel free to use chicken thighs or legs instead of breasts.

2 tablespoons garlic powder
1 tablespoon sugar
2 teaspoons ground ancho chile pepper
2 teaspoons salt
1 teaspoon ground allspice
1 teaspoon thyme
1 teaspoon sage
1 teaspoon ground nutmeg
1 teaspoon ground cinnamon
1 teaspoon black pepper

¾ cup white vinegar
½ cup orange juice, preferably freshly squeezed
¼ cup olive oil
¼ cup soy sauce
2 tablespoons freshly squeezed lime juice
1 cup chopped white onion
3 green onions, finely chopped
1½ pounds boneless, skinless chicken breasts

Combine the garlic powder, sugar, ancho chile, salt, allspice, thyme, sage, nutmeg, cinnamon, and pepper in a medium bowl. Whisk in the vinegar, orange juice, olive oil, soy sauce, and lime juice. Stir in the white and green onions. Measure out ½ cup of the marinade and set aside. Add the chicken to the remaining marinade, cover, and marinate in the refrigerator for 1 hour.

Preheat the grill to medium. Place the chicken on the grill and discard the used marinade. Grill the chicken, brushing with the reserved marinade, until the chicken is thoroughly cooked and the internal temperature reaches 165°F.

Serves 4 to 6

The Dutch were so eager to monopolize the nutmeg business that they traded the island of New Amsterdam to the British in exchange for Run, a tiny nutmeg island in the Moluccas. Today, New Amsterdam is better known as Manhattan.

Tandoori Chicken Skewers  with Curry Butter Sauce

Round up the spices—these chicken chunks are begging for a flavor medley. The tandoori marinade is a treat in itself. Add the Curry Butter Sauce and your entrée is complete.

½ cup plain low-fat yogurt
2 cloves garlic, minced
2 teaspoons ground ancho chile pepper
2 teaspoons ground cumin
2 teaspoons ground coriander
1 teaspoon ground ginger

1 teaspoon ground turmeric
1 teaspoon dried lemon zest
1 teaspoon kosher salt
1½ pounds boneless, skinless chicken thighs, cut into chunks
1 cup Curry Butter Sauce (recipe follows)

Soak 4 to 6 bamboo skewers in a shallow dish of water. Combine the yogurt, garlic, ancho chile, cumin, coriander, ginger, turmeric, lemon zest, and salt in a large bowl. Add the chicken to the yogurt marinade and stir until the chicken is thoroughly coated. Cover the bowl and marinate the chicken in the refrigerator for 1 hour.

Preheat the grill to medium. Carefully thread the chicken pieces onto the skewers. Grill the chicken skewers, turning occasionally, until the internal temperature reaches 165°F, 6 to 8 minutes. Serve immediately with the butter sauce for dipping.

Serves 4

Turmeric is a member of the ginger family. Most of the world's turmeric is grown and consumed in India, where it is used as a flavoring, a dye, and a medicine.

Curry Butter Sauce

• •

This butter sauce is delicious with the Tandoori Chicken Skewers, but you'll find plenty of other uses for it as well. The key to this sauce is to not melt the butter completely.

½ cup white wine
¼ cup white wine vinegar
¼ cup finely minced shallots
2 tablespoons Curry Spice Blend (recipe follows)
2 tablespoons heavy cream
16 tablespoons (2 sticks) cold, unsalted butter
¼ cup chopped fresh cilantro
Kosher salt

Combine the wine, vinegar, shallots, and curry spice blend in a small saucepan. Bring to a simmer over medium heat, stirring continually, and reduce the liquid until the pan is almost dry. Stir in the cream and cook for 2 minutes. Remove the saucepan from the heat and whisk in the cold butter 2 tablespoons at a time. (Place the sauce over very low heat only as needed to soften the butter. Do not let the butter completely melt as it will separate.) Stir the cilantro into the sauce and season with salt to taste. Serve immediately.

Makes 1 cup

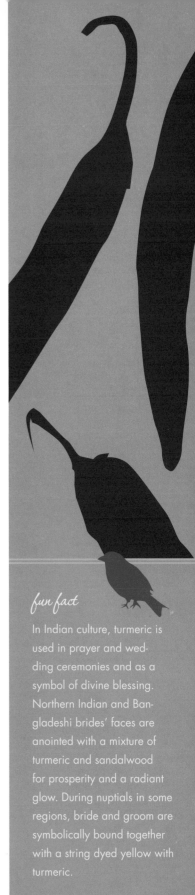

fun fact

In Indian culture, turmeric is used in prayer and wedding ceremonies and as a symbol of divine blessing. Northern Indian and Bangladeshi brides' faces are anointed with a mixture of turmeric and sandalwood for prosperity and a radiant glow. During nuptials in some regions, bride and groom are symbolically bound together with a string dyed yellow with turmeric.

Curry Spice Blend

• •

Curry is a blend of spices, a mixture that in India is endlessly tweaked to individual preferences. We like this formula. Use it to flavor mayonnaise, sour cream, or sauces. You can also add it to vegetables or rice. Its uses are limited only by your imagination.

2 teaspoons ground cumin
1 teaspoon ground coriander
1 teaspoon ground ginger
1 teaspoon ground turmeric
1 teaspoon ground mild chile pepper

Combine all the ingredients for the seasoning in a small bowl. Store the unused seasoning in an airtight container for up to 2 months.

Makes 2 tablespoons

Note: *Use this blend to flavor mayonnaise for salads or sandwiches. As a general rule, start with 1 teaspoon of the curry mixture for ½ cup of mayonnaise or other sauce, and add more if you like.*

Turmeric, or haldi, is a main ingredient of curry mixtures. Its musky aroma serves as a base to show off the flavors of other spices. It is named after the French terre-mérite (after the Latin *terra merita*, or "meritorious earth"), probably because in powdered form it looks like yellow ocher, a pigment used by painters.

Coconut Curry Shrimp

It's easy to forget that curry is a blend of spices, not a single flavor. One of the virtues of this coconut curry shrimp is that it allows you to blend your own curry—so feel free to tweak the spice blend to your own personal curry preference. The main virtue of this dish will be obvious when you serve it and watch it disappear with record speed. You might need to issue some plate-licking permits.

2 tablespoons olive oil
2 cups diced onion (any variety)
6 cloves garlic, minced
2 tablespoons Curry Spice Blend (page 119)
1 cup chicken broth
¼ cup apricot preserves
1 (14-ounce) can unsweetened coconut milk
1 pound uncooked medium shrimp, peeled,
**   and deveined**
¼ cup fresh lime juice
¼ cup chopped fresh cilantro
Salt and black pepper
Steamed rice (optional)

Heat the oil in a large skillet over medium heat. Add the onion to the oil and sauté until tender, about 5 minutes. Add the garlic and curry spice blend and cook, stirring continually, for 1 minute. Add the chicken broth and apricot preserves and cook, stirring often, for 10 minutes. Increase the heat to medium-high, stir in the coconut milk and simmer, stirring often, until the curry reaches the desired thickness, about 10 minutes. Add the shrimp and cook, stirring occasionally, until the shrimp are pink and just cooked through, about 2 minutes. Stir in the lime juice and cilantro and season with salt and pepper to taste. Serve the coconut curry shrimp over steamed rice, if using.

Serves 4

| Steak (with) Marinade |

• •

Why buy a premixed marinade or steak rub when it's easier to make your own and the results are so much better? This marinade will convince you that doing it yourself with full-flavored organic spices is the only way to go.

1 cup finely minced onion (any variety)
⅔ cup red wine vinegar
2 tablespoons minced garlic
2 teaspoons sugar
2 teaspoons oregano
2 teaspoons ground cumin
1 teaspoon thyme
½ teaspoon salt
½ teaspoon black pepper
⅔ cup oil
4 steaks of choice

Whisk together the onion, vinegar, garlic, sugar, oregano, cumin, thyme, salt, and pepper in a small bowl. Add the oil in a slow, steady stream, whisking constantly, until blended. Measure out ¼ cup of the marinade and set aside. Pour the remaining marinade into a large resealable plastic bag. Add the steak to the marinade, seal the bag, and marinate in the refrigerator for 4 hours.

Preheat the grill to medium. Place the steaks on the grill and discard the used marinade. Grill the steaks, brushing with the reserved ¼ cup of the marinade, to the desired doneness.

Serves 4

As late as 1937, Cornish subjects presented King George VI with "quit-rents" that freed them from the obligation of feudal service. This symbolic tax included a traditional pound of cumin.

Filet Mignon (with) Green Peppercorn Sauce

Chefs have paired tarragon with fine pieces of beef for centuries, and we love what this aromatic herb can do to a peppercorn sauce. We've paired it here with filet mignon, but it works beautifully on grilled steak as well.

4 (5-ounce) beef tenderloin steaks, about 1 inch thick
Kosher salt
2 tablespoons canola or other mild-tasting oil
1 tablespoon butter
1 tablespoon minced shallots
1 clove garlic, minced
¼ cup red wine
1 cup heavy cream
1 tablespoon green peppercorns in brine, drained
2 teaspoons tarragon
Salt and black pepper

Pat the steaks dry and season with kosher salt. Heat the oil in a medium skillet over medium heat. Add the steaks and cook, turning once, until the steaks reach the desired doneness. Remove the steaks from the skillet and let stand, loosely covered, for 10 minutes. (The steaks will continue to cook as they stand.)

While the steak is resting, warm the butter in the same skillet over medium heat. Add the shallots and sauté until tender. Add the garlic and cook, stirring continually, for 1 minute. Pour in the wine and bring to a boil over high heat. Decrease the heat to medium and stir in the cream, peppercorns, and tarragon. Cook the sauce, stirring occasionally, until thickened, about 10 minutes. Stir in any meat drippings that have collected from the resting steaks and season with salt and pepper to taste. Serve the warm steaks topped with the green peppercorn sauce.

Serves 4

Tarragon has been used to cure hiccups and get rid of worms; it was also thought to cure snakebite and rabies.

Spiced Orange Pan Sauce over Grilled Lamb

If you love what a strong herb like rosemary can do for lamb, you'll be delighted with the rounded flavors of this spiced sauce. Once you try it, we suspect you'll be putting lamb on the menu much more often.

1 tablespoon olive oil
⅓ cup minced shallots
4 teaspoons sugar
2 teaspoons ground cumin
1 teaspoon ground cinnamon
1 teaspoon ground green cardamom
⅓ cup red wine vinegar
½ cup orange juice
3 cups chicken broth
1½ to 2 pounds lamb chops
1 clove garlic, smashed and peeled
Salt and black pepper

Preheat the grill to medium. Heat the oil in a medium skillet over medium heat. Add the shallots to the oil and sauté until tender, about 2 minutes. Stir in the sugar, cumin, cinnamon, and cardamom and cook for 1 minute. Increase the heat to medium-high and pour in the vinegar to deglaze the pan. Stir in the orange juice and cook for 2 minutes. Add the chicken broth and cook, stirring frequently, until the sauce thickens and reduces to ¾ cup, about 15 to 20 minutes.

While the sauce is cooking, rub both sides of each lamb chop with the smashed garlic clove. Season the lamb with salt and pepper. Grill the lamb chops to desired doneness. Serve the lamb chops topped with the spiced orange pan sauce.

Serves 4 to 6

Spice-Rubbed Rack of Lamb

• •

The balance of herbs and spices in this rub complements and enhances the succulent flavors of lamb.

4 cloves garlic, minced
1 large shallot, minced
2 teaspoons rosemary
2 teaspoons thyme
1 teaspoon dried orange zest
1 teaspoon ground allspice
1 teaspoon coarse salt
1 teaspoon black pepper
2 tablespoons olive oil
2 (1 to 1½ pounds each) racks of lamb

Preheat the oven to 475°F. Combine the garlic, shallot, rosemary, thyme, orange zest, allspice, salt, and pepper in a small bowl. Stir in the oil. Spread the rub evenly over all sides of the lamb and rub into the meat.

Place the lamb, bone side down, in a roasting pan. Roast for 10 minutes. Decrease the oven temperature to 375°F and continue roasting for an additional 10 minutes. Turn the oven off, leave the oven door closed, and let the lamb stand in the hot oven for 10 minutes. Remove the lamb from the oven. To serve, carve the lamb into chops by cutting between the bones.

Serves 4 to 6

A Viennese manuscript of 1235 lists rosemary, myrtle, and lavender infused in wine as ingredients of "Hungary water." The concoction gained fame, and its name, when it was credited with curing the Queen of Hungary's paralysis.

fun fact

Thyme is known to lure bees— and fairies. Gardeners once used thyme in orchards to attract the bees needed to pollinate fruit trees; but beds of thyme were also planted outside homes to provide fairy lodgings.

| Side Dishes |

Even the best entrées need a supporting cast—and, as vegetable lovers, we're delighted when side dishes steal the show. That can easily happen when familiar foods are judiciously enhanced with a teaspoon or two of organic herbs or spices.

In this chapter, we offer some simple ways to spice up old favorites like roasted potatoes or to turn healthy-but-boring choices like cauliflower into family favorites. If you're looking for more ways to eat vegetables, try the roasted cauliflower dish as an appetizer—a tasty change from high-fat chips and dips.

We also started thinking about comfort foods, and we couldn't help but revisit some food memories from our childhood. Katie's mother's cornbread has become a staple in her kitchen, and it's a perfect vehicle for various combinations of spices and herbs. Sara always looks for ways to spice up other Southern favorites—hence a new version of baked garlic cheese grits. Call it polenta, and you'll think it's haute cuisine. And let's not forget those vegetable salads of the 1950s, '60s, and '70s, often featuring canned goods and mayonnaise. We've updated one of Katie's favorites from that era, Green Pea Salad.

Remember, these recipes are templates. Use them as inspiration to find your own favorite flavor combinations. You might find yourself thinking of side dishes as the real stars of the show.

Green Pea Salad

Katie's mother loved to make green pea salad with canned peas, unremarkable cheddar, and lots of mayonnaise. We've upgraded the ingredients, added some interesting flavors, and created a recipe that holds more than sentiment.

1 (14-ounce) package frozen peas, thawed but not cooked
¾ cup feta cheese, crumbled
3 shallots, finely diced
5 to 6 tablespoons mayonnaise
1 teaspoon tarragon
1 teaspoon fennel seed
1 teaspoon dried lemon zest
Salt and black pepper

In a medium bowl, combine the peas, feta, and shallots. In a small bowl, mix together the mayonnaise, tarragon, fennel seeds, and lemon zest. Stir the mayonnaise mixture into the pea mixture. Add salt and pepper to taste.

Variation: Substitute sharp cheddar, diced to about the size of peas, for the feta, and ground mild chile pepper for the tarragon.

Serves 6 to 8

According to the *Kama Sutra*, a mixture of fennel, ghee (clarified butter), sugar, honey, milk, and licorice acts as a sweet sexual tonic.

Toasting Hazelnuts

Hazelnuts can be purchased both skinned and unskinned. We prefer skinned hazelnuts for this recipe, mostly for looks. To toast skinned and chopped hazelnuts, place a rack in the middle of the oven and preheat the oven to 350°F. Spread the nuts on a baking sheet and toast for about 5 minutes, or until they just begin to turn golden brown and fragrant. There is a fine line between toasting nuts and burning them, so pay attention!

If you're using unskinned hazelnuts, you'll want to start with about ⅓ cup of whole nuts. To toast the whole nuts, place them in the middle of a 350°F oven for 10 to 12 minutes, or until they become fragrant and the skins begin to crack and peel away from the nuts. Again, watch them carefully to avoid burning.

To remove some of the skins, place the freshly toasted nuts in a clean kitchen towel, fold the towel over the nuts, and rub the nuts vigorously in the towel. It's fine if some of the skins remain on the nuts. Let the hazelnuts cool completely before chopping them.

Butternut Squash and Sage Risotto

We love risotto—not just the creamy finished product, but also the process of making it. There's something about gently coaxing moisture into each grain of rice that is supremely satisfying. Maybe it's because the process reminds us that some things can't be rushed. We also love the results and the many variations. This one, featuring butternut squash, is among our all-time favorites—probably because it stars sage, one of our very favorite herbs.

This risotto is an elegant accompaniment to an autumn dinner. With a salad, it could also serve as the centerpiece of a vegetarian meal.

3 cups chicken or vegetable broth or stock
2 tablespoons butter
2 cups chopped yellow onion
4 cups peeled and cubed butternut squash
   (½-inch cubes)
1 teaspoon sage
½ cup Arborio or medium-grain rice
½ cup dry white wine
⅓ cup freshly grated Parmesan cheese
¼ cup chopped hazelnuts, toasted (see page 130)
Salt and coarse black pepper

Bring the broth to a simmer in a small saucepan over medium heat. Decrease the heat to low and keep the broth warm.

Melt the butter in a medium-size, heavy saucepan over medium heat. Add the onion and sauté until tender, about 8 minutes. Add the squash and sage and continue to sauté for an additional 2 minutes. Cover and cook until the squash is tender, about 6 minutes.

Stir in the rice and cook until a white spot appears in the center of the grains, about 2 minutes. Add the wine and simmer, stirring continuously, until the liquid is absorbed. Add the broth, 1 cup at a time, and continue simmering and stirring until the liquid is absorbed before adding the next cup. Stir in the Parmesan cheese and hazelnuts and season with salt and pepper to taste, about ½ teaspoon each.

Serves 6

Rosemary Roasted Potato Medley

You can't go wrong with roasted potatoes. Served warm on a cold night or cold at a summer lunch—they have a way of making a meal complete. This simple preparation features rosemary, but a combination of herbs or spices works well, too.

**1 pound sweet potatoes, peeled and
    cut into 1-inch cubes**
1 pound red potatoes, cut into 1-inch cubes
2 tablespoons olive oil
2 cloves garlic, minced
2 teaspoons rosemary
1 teaspoon coarse salt

Preheat the oven to 425°F. Place the sweet potatoes and red potatoes into a large roasting pan. Drizzle the olive oil over the potatoes and toss the potatoes until thoroughly coated. Add the garlic, rosemary, and salt and gently toss to coat. Roast the potatoes, stirring occasionally, until browned and crisped, about 30 minutes. Serve the roasted potatoes hot out of the oven or at room temperature.

Serves 4 to 6

Variations: *Instead of 2 teaspoons of rosemary, use one of the following combinations:*
1 teaspoon of thyme and 1 teaspoon of rosemary
Or
1 teaspoon of ground cumin and 1 teaspoon of ground coriander. If you like a touch of heat, add 1 teaspoon of ground mild chile pepper.

A 1699 English cookbook recommends rosemary as "always welcome in Vinegar; but above all, a fresh Sprig or two in a Glass of Wine."

Marjoram Mashed Potatoes

●●●

The secret to good mashed potatoes is to use the right potato, and we think there's none better for the purpose than Yukon gold. Marjoram, with a gentler flavor than its cousin oregano, adds a light herbal note.

1½ pounds Yukon gold potatoes, peeled
1 tablespoon kosher salt
4 tablespoons (½ stick) butter
¼ to ⅓ cup heavy cream, warmed
1 teaspoon marjoram
Salt and black pepper

Cut the potatoes into 1½-inch cubes. Place the potatoes and salt in a large pot of water. Bring the water to a boil, then lower the heat and simmer for 15 minutes, or until the potatoes are tender when pierced with a fork. Drain the potatoes in a colander and then return to the saucepan. Mash the potatoes using a potato masher, ricer, or food mill. Stir the butter into the mashed potatoes. Add the warmed cream and marjoram and stir until completely absorbed. Season the mashed potatoes with salt and pepper to taste and serve hot.

Serves 4

Baked Sweet Potato Steak Fries

Sweet, spicy, and altogether tantalizing, these oven "fries" are proof that there need be nothing junky about fast and easy food.

2 pounds sweet potatoes, unpeeled
3 tablespoons olive oil
1 teaspoon ground coriander
1 teaspoon oregano
1 teaspoon ground mild chile pepper
1 teaspoon fennel seed
1 teaspoon kosher salt

Preheat the oven to 450°F. Slice the potatoes lengthwise into 1-inch wedges. Place the sweet potatoes into a large roasting pan. Drizzle the olive oil over the potatoes and toss the potatoes until thoroughly coated. In a small bowl, combine the coriander, oregano, mild chile pepper, fennel seed, and salt. Sprinkle the seasoning mixture over the potatoes and gently toss to coat. Place the roasting pan in the middle of the oven and bake the potatoes for 15 minutes. Remove the pan from the oven and turn the potato wedges over with a spatula. Return the pan to the oven and bake an additional 15 to 20 minutes, or until the potatoes are tender and slightly browned. Serve the sweet potato fries hot out of the oven or at room temperature.

Serves 4 to 6

In early America, the Puritans brought dill, fennel, and other seeds to church to chew during long sermons. These seeds became known as "meeting seeds."

Grilled Asparagus Spears

 with

Lemon-Cumin Beurre Blanc Sauce

• •

Grilled asparagus is a seasonal favorite in our households, and there's no better way to enjoy it than with a cumin-laced beurre blanc.

1 pound asparagus spears, trimmed
2 tablespoons olive oil
Salt
½ cup Lemon-Cumin Beurre Blanc Sauce (recipe follows)

Preheat the grill to high. Place the asparagus in a shallow dish. Drizzle the olive oil over the asparagus and toss the spears until lightly coated. Grill the asparagus over medium heat, turning frequently, until the spears are just tender, about 5 minutes. Remove from the grill and season with salt to taste. Arrange the asparagus on a platter and serve with beurre blanc sauce. Serve immediately.

Serves 4

Lemon-Cumin Beurre Blanc Sauce

● ●

The French term beurre blanc means "white butter," and it's a technique worth mastering. Infuse it with the earthy appeal of cumin and it takes on a global sophistication. It's great with fish, chicken, or vegetables. We especially love what it can do for one of our favorite vegetable treats, grilled asparagus.

¼ cup white wine
2 tablespoons freshly squeezed lemon juice
2 cloves garlic, minced
1 to 2 teaspoons ground cumin
8 tablespoons (1 stick) cold, unsalted butter
Kosher salt

Combine the wine, lemon juice, garlic, and cumin in a small saucepan. Bring to a simmer over medium heat and cook, stirring continually, until reduced by three-quarters. Remove from the heat and whisk in the cold butter, 1 tablespoon at a time. (Place the sauce over very low heat only as needed to soften the butter. Do not let the butter completely melt as it will separate.) Season the sauce with salt to taste, about ¼ teaspoon. Serve immediately.

Makes ½ cup

Note: *The key is to not let the butter melt completely.*

fun fact

Cumin seeds have been found in the pyramids, interred with the pharaohs of ancient Egypt.

Roasted Spiced Cauliflower

Cauliflower may seem an unlikely candidate for a fancy side dish. But spice it up and roast it, and you'll find its hidden appeal. This makes a delicious appetizer as well.

1 pound cauliflower, cut into 1-inch florets
2 tablespoons extra-virgin olive oil
1 teaspoon ground cumin
1 teaspoon ground coriander
Salt and black pepper
2 tablespoons pine nuts
⅓ cup green olives, pitted and chopped
1 tablespoon drained capers

Preheat the oven to 425°F. In a roasting pan, toss the cauliflower with the olive oil and season with cumin, coriander, and salt and pepper. Roast for 20 minutes, or until the cauliflower begins to brown. Add the pine nuts, olives, and capers, then toss and roast for another 10 minutes, or until the pine nuts are lightly toasted. Serve immediately or at room temperature.

Serves 4 to 6

Italian Herb Vegetable Casserole

The key to this casserole is slicing all the vegetables the same thickness. Use a sharp knife, a mandoline, or a food processor with the slicing disk attached. This medley of vegetable flavors is a dish you'll want to return to again and again.

3 red potatoes, thinly sliced into rounds
1 small zucchini, thinly sliced into rounds
1 small yellow crookneck squash, thinly sliced into rounds
2 tablespoons plus 1 tablespoon olive oil
1 teaspoon rosemary
1 teaspoon thyme
1 teaspoon garlic powder
1 teaspoon kosher salt
½ small onion (any variety), thinly sliced into rounds
1 large Roma tomato, thinly sliced into rounds
½ cup freshly grated Parmesan cheese
¼ cup plain breadcrumbs
1 teaspoon basil

Preheat the oven to 400°F. Grease an 8-inch square or round baking dish. Place the potatoes, zucchini, and squash into a medium bowl. Drizzle 2 tablespoons of the oil over the vegetables and toss until thoroughly coated. In a small bowl, combine the rosemary, thyme, garlic powder, and salt. Sprinkle the seasoning mixture over the vegetables and gently toss to coat. Layer the vegetables in the baking dish. Arrange the onion slices evenly over the layered vegetables. Arrange the tomato slices on top of the onion.

Combine the Parmesan cheese, breadcrumbs, and basil in a small bowl. Stir in the remaining 1 tablespoon of oil and toss to combine. Evenly sprinkle the breadcrumb mixture on top of the tomato slices. Bake the casserole until the vegetables are tender and the topping is golden brown, about 40 minutes.

Serves 6

Basil's association with love figures in the tale of Lisabetta from Boccaccio's *Decameron*, which later inspired a Keats poem and became a popular subject for prints.

Black Beans (with) Tomatoes and Spices

Beans are good for you, but they can also be just plain good. We love this southwestern-flavored version of black beans and tomatoes. It's a great side dish, but you can also top it with shredded cheese and eat it as a main course.

1½ cups (10½ ounces) dried black beans, soaked
  overnight in cold water and drained
1 tablespoon vegetable oil
1 medium onion (any variety), finely chopped
4 cloves garlic, minced
2 medium tomatoes, coarsely chopped, or 1 (14-ounce)
  can chopped tomatoes
2 teaspoons ground mild chile pepper
1 teaspoon oregano
1 teaspoon ground cumin
1 teaspoon ground coriander
1 teaspoon dried lemon zest
Salt and black pepper

In a large saucepan, cover the beans with 2 inches of water and bring to a boil. Reduce the heat to low and simmer for 1 hour, stirring occasionally. Meanwhile, in a medium skillet, heat the vegetable oil. Add the onion and garlic and cook over moderate heat until softened.

Add the onion and garlic mixture to the beans, along with the tomatoes, chile pepper, oregano, cumin, coriander, lemon zest, and enough water to cover. Season to taste with salt and pepper and continue simmering until the beans are tender, up to 2 hours. Check occasionally and replenish the water if necessary.

Serves 6 to 8

Buttermilk Potato Salad  Fennel and Dill

Fennel seed, dill weed, and lemon zest combine to work magic in this dressed-up version of that old favorite, potato salad.

3 pounds red potatoes, cut into eighths
1 tablespoon plus ¾ teaspoon kosher salt
½ cup buttermilk
⅓ cup sour cream
⅓ cup mayonnaise
4 scallions, thinly sliced
1 teaspoon fennel seed
1 teaspoon dill weed
1 teaspoon dried lemon zest
¾ teaspoon coarse black pepper

Place the potatoes and 1 tablespoon of the salt in a large pot of water. Bring the water to a boil, then lower the heat and simmer for 10 to 15 minutes, until the potatoes are barely tender when pierced with a knife. Drain the potatoes in a colander and allow the potatoes to cool to room temperature.

While the potatoes are cooling, whisk together the buttermilk, sour cream, mayonnaise, scallions, fennel seed, dill weed, lemon zest, pepper, and the remaining ¾ teaspoon salt. Place the potatoes in a large bowl. Pour the dressing over the potatoes and gently toss to coat. Cover and refrigerate for 2 hours to allow the flavors to blend. Serve the potato salad cold or at room temperature.

Serves 6 to 8

Henry Wadsworth Longfellow referred to fennel's miraculous properties (and military uses) in his poem "The Goblet of Life":

"Above the lowly plant it towers,
The fennel, with its yellow flowers,
And in an earlier age than ours
Was gifted with the wondrous powers,
Lost vision to restore.

It gave new strength, and fearless mood;
And gladiators, fierce and rude,
Mingled it in their daily food;
And he who battled and subdued,
A wreath of fennel wore."

Baked Garlic Cheese Grits

● ●

No longer just for breakfast, grits have been showing up at the dinner table in recent years in dishes like shrimp and grits, or disguised as polenta, the Italian version of the old Southern favorite. Grits and polenta are both basically just ground corn. This recipe makes a great side dish for casual suppers.

4 cups water
1 cup yellow corn grits
2 cloves garlic, minced
1 teaspoon salt
8 ounces Monterey Jack cheese, grated
5 ounces Parmesan cheese, grated
4 tablespoons (½ stick) butter, melted
3 eggs
1 teaspoon oregano
1 teaspoon ground mild chile pepper
½ teaspoon black pepper

Preheat the oven to 350°F and grease an 8-inch square or round baking dish. Combine the water, grits, garlic, and salt in a large saucepan. Bring the grits to a boil over high heat, stirring constantly. Decrease the heat, cover, and simmer the grits for 5 minutes or until thickened.

Remove the saucepan from the heat. Add the Monterey Jack and Parmesan cheeses and stir until the cheese melts. In a small bowl, whisk together the butter and eggs. Add the egg mixture to the grits and stir until thoroughly combined. Stir in the oregano, chile pepper, and black pepper.

Pour the grits into the baking dish and bake for 1 hour or until the grits are set. Let cool for 10 minutes before slicing and serving.

Serves 6 to 9

Coconut Red-Lentil Curry

• •

Lentils are delicious and nutritious. This curried version calls for red lentils, but you can substitute other kinds as well. These lentils are a good side dish, but they can also serve as a main course for a meatless meal.

1 medium onion (any variety), finely chopped
2 tablespoons vegetable oil
2 teaspoons ground ginger
2 cloves garlic, finely chopped
1 teaspoon ground cumin
1 teaspoon ground coriander
1 teaspoon ground turmeric
1 teaspoon ground mild chile pepper
1 teaspoon salt, plus additional for seasoning
2 cups water
1½ cups dried red lentils (10 ounces)
1 (13- to 14-ounce) can unsweetened coconut milk
1 pound zucchini (2 medium, cut into ¼-inch dice)
1 cup loosely packed cilantro sprigs, for garnish
Steamed Basmati rice, for serving

Sauté the onion in the oil in a 3½- to 4-quart heavy pot over moderate heat, stirring occasionally, until the edges are golden, about 6 minutes. Add ginger and garlic and cook, stirring, for 1 minute. Add the cumin, coriander, turmeric, chile pepper, and 1 teaspoon of the salt. Cook, stirring, for 1 minute.

Stir in the water, lentils, and coconut milk. Cover the pot and simmer for 5 minutes, stirring occasionally. Stir in the zucchini, cover the pot again, and simmer until the lentils and zucchini are tender, about 15 minutes for red lentils (cooking times may vary with other types of lentils).

Season with salt and serve with cilantro sprigs scattered on top. Serve with rice.

Serves 6

Parmesan Herb Scones

Scones are a great vehicle for herbs and spices. We love the way these savory scones meld the flavors of several herbs. Topped with sautéed onion, they are a tasty accompaniment to any meal, whether a fancy dinner or a comforting bowl of soup.

3 cups all-purpose flour
1 cup freshly grated Parmesan cheese
4 teaspoons baking powder
1 teaspoon oregano
1 teaspoon basil
¾ teaspoon salt
½ teaspoon garlic powder
½ teaspoon baking soda

6 tablespoons cold unsalted butter
1 egg
1 cup buttermilk
2 tablespoons cold unsalted butter
1 medium onion (any variety), thinly sliced
1 teaspoon rosemary
½ teaspoon thyme

Preheat the oven to 425°F and grease a large baking sheet. Combine the flour, cheese, baking powder, oregano, basil, salt, garlic powder, and baking soda in a large bowl. Using a pastry blender or two knives cut in 6 tablespoons of the butter, until the butter is the size of small crumbs.

Whisk together the egg and buttermilk in a small bowl. Add the mixture to the dry ingredients and stir until just combined. Turn the dough out onto a lightly floured surface. Handling the dough as little as possible, knead the dough 5 to 6 times.

Divide the dough in half and form two round balls. Place both onto the baking sheet and flatten into 8-inch circles. Score the dough, and divide each circle into six equal wedges.

To make the topping, melt the remaining 2 tablespoons of butter in a medium skillet over medium-high heat. Add the onion and sauté until tender. Stir in the rosemary and thyme. Spread the mixture evenly over the two dough rounds.

Bake the scones for 20 to 25 minutes, until the top is golden brown. Cut into wedges and serve.

Makes 12 scones

Pear Cardamom Bread

If you've never known why cardamom is called the Queen of Spices, this bread is for you. Cardamom's exquisite sweetness is the perfect complement to the elegant pear. Caution: you might want to double this recipe; one loaf won't be enough.

1⅔ cups all-purpose flour
1½ teaspoons baking powder
¾ teaspoon salt
2 eggs
¾ cup sugar
1 teaspoon ground green cardamom
1 teaspoon dried orange zest
½ cup vegetable oil
¼ cup milk
1½ cups chopped, unpeeled pears,
    any variety (about 2 pears)

Topping

1 teaspoon sugar
½ to 1 teaspoon ground green cardamom

Preheat the oven to 350°F and grease the bottom of a loaf pan.

Whisk the flour, baking powder, and salt together in a large bowl. In a small bowl, whisk the eggs, add the sugar, and whisk another minute or two. Add the cardamom, orange zest, oil, and milk to the egg mixture and stir. Combine the egg mixture with the flour mixture, then fold in the pears. Pour the batter into the prepared pan. For the topping, sprinkle the sugar-cardamom mixture on top and bake for 55 to 65 minutes, or until a toothpick inserted in the middle comes out clean.

Remove the pan from the oven and allow the loaf to cool for 10 minutes, then remove the loaf from the pan and allow it to cool for about 1 hour before slicing.

Makes 1 loaf

fun fact

In India, the first taste of solid food for many infants is cardamom-scented rice. In the sweet kitchens of Sweden, bakers prefer cardamom to cinnamon.

Katie's Cornbread

• •

This is a traditional Texas-style cornbread, crusty and not sweet. You can make it plain, or you can add any herb or savory spice you like, from extra chile to fennel seed to ginger and even allspice. It's good by itself, but it's heavenly with butter.

1 cup yellow cornmeal
½ cup all-purpose flour
1 teaspoon salt
1 tablespoon baking powder
½ teaspoon baking soda
1 teaspoon ground mild chile pepper **or**
ancho chile pepper
1 cup buttermilk
½ cup whole milk
1 egg
¼ cup melted shortening or canola oil

Preheat the oven to 450°F. Coat a 10-inch skillet with ¼ inch of vegetable oil and place the skillet on high heat on a stovetop burner.

Combine the cornmeal, flour, salt, baking powder, baking soda, and chile pepper and mix thoroughly. Add the buttermilk, milk, egg, and shortening and gently combine. Do not overmix.

When the skillet is hot, carefully pour in the batter. (Be careful, as the batter may splatter when it comes into contact with the hot oil.)

Put the skillet in the oven and cook, uncovered, 30 to 40 minutes, or until golden brown and crispy. Let cool slightly, and turn out onto a serving plate or platter.

Makes 1 (10-inch) loaf

In his multivolume survey of Aztec knowledge and customs, sixteenth-century Franciscan friar Bernardino de Sahagún worked with Nahuatl-speaking assistants and recorded the names of nearly 40 kinds of chile peppers.

Dill Cornbread

• •

If you've never been a fan of cornbread, you may change your mind when the aroma of this bread wafts through the house. In fact, we've heard it called "finger-lickin' good"—and that's a huge compliment from cornbread purists. This cornbread uses equal portions of cornmeal and flour, giving it wide appeal.

1 cup yellow cornmeal
1 cup all-purpose flour
⅓ cup sugar
2 teaspoons dill weed
1½ teaspoons baking powder
1 teaspoon salt
½ teaspoon baking soda
1 cup buttermilk
¼ cup canola or other mild-tasting oil
1 egg

Preheat the oven to 425°F and grease an 8-inch square or round baking pan. Combine the cornmeal, flour, sugar, dill, baking powder, salt, and baking soda in a medium bowl. In a small bowl, whisk together the buttermilk, oil, and egg. Add the buttermilk mixture to the cornmeal mixture and stir until just combined. Spoon the batter into the prepared pan and bake for 15 minutes, or until golden brown.

Makes 1 (8-inch) loaf

fun fact

English poet Michael Drayton referred to the widespread belief that dill protected against witchcraft when he wrote in 1627, "Therewith her Veruayne and her Dill, That hindreth Witches of their will."

Savory French Bread

• •

When you're in the mood for something more than plain bread and butter, try this herbed and cheesy treat.

1 cup mayonnaise
1 cup freshly grated Parmesan cheese
½ cup diced white or yellow onion
1 teaspoon Worcestershire sauce
1 teaspoon marjoram
1 teaspoon oregano
2 cloves garlic
¼ teaspoon kosher salt
1 loaf of French bread, split in half lengthwise

Preheat the oven to 350°F. Combine the mayonnaise, Parmesan, onion, Worcestershire, marjoram, oregano, garlic, and salt in a food processor. Pulse the mayonnaise mixture, scraping down the sides of the bowl, until smooth. Spread half of the mixture evenly over each half loaf. Bake the bread, spread side up, on the oven rack until bubbly and golden, 15 to 18 minutes. Slice the bread with a serrated knife and serve hot.

Makes 1 loaf

Oregano is versatile outside the kitchen, too: Like its milder cousin marjoram, oregano is associated with marital bliss and is woven into crowns for Greek newlyweds, but it's also customarily planted on graves to ensure the happiness of the deceased.

Zucchini Bread

If you've ever planted zucchini and reached a point in the summer harvest when you didn't know what to do with all the bounty, zucchini bread is for you. Even if you don't grow your own, this recipe will make the green squash a regular on your shopping list.

This version of zucchini bread is moist and tasty, with nutmeg lending a sweetly spiced aftertaste. We think you'll enjoy the full teaspoon of nutmeg, but if you or the folks you're feeding are spice shy, use ½ teaspoon the first time you make it. You'll soon crave more.

1½ cups all-purpose flour

2 teaspoons ground cinnamon

1 teaspoon dried lemon zest

½ to 1 teaspoon ground nutmeg

½ teaspoon baking soda

½ teaspoon salt

¼ teaspoon baking powder

1 egg

¼ cup canola or other mild-tasting oil

1 cup sugar

1 cup finely shredded unpeeled zucchini

1 cup chopped walnuts

Preheat the oven to 350°F and grease a 9 by 5-inch loaf pan. Sift together the flour, cinnamon, lemon zest, nutmeg, baking soda, salt, and baking powder into a large mixing bowl. In a small mixing bowl, whisk together the egg and oil. Stir in the sugar. Add the zucchini to the liquid ingredients and stir to combine. Add the zucchini mixture to the flour mixture and stir until just combined. Fold in the walnuts.

Pour the batter into the prepared pan and bake for 50 to 60 minutes, until a toothpick inserted in the center comes out clean. Allow the bread to cool in the pan for 10 minutes, then remove it from the pan and place it on a rack to cool for about 1 hour before slicing.

Makes 1 loaf

Thirteenth-century English friar Roger Bacon, a scientist and philosopher, recommended a mixture of chopped viper, cloves, nutmeg, and mace to fight aging.

Fennel Seed Soda Bread Rolls

Inspired by Irish soda bread, these rolls feature the alluring aroma of fennel seeds and will be the talk of your table. Serve them plain or with Marjoram Shallot Butter.

8 tablespoons (1 stick) butter, at room temperature
3 tablespoons sugar
1 egg
3½ cups all-purpose flour
1 teaspoon baking soda
1 teaspoon salt
1¼ cups buttermilk
2 teaspoons fennel seed

Preheat the oven to 400°F. Grease a large baking sheet. Cream the butter and sugar in a food processor fitted with a steel blade until light and fluffy. Add in the egg and mix until thoroughly combined. Sift the flour, baking soda, and salt into a medium bowl. Add half of the flour mixture to the butter mixture and pulse until combined. Add the remaining half of the flour mixture and gradually pour in the buttermilk while mixing. Continue mixing the dough until the machine slows down.

Turn the dough out onto a lightly floured surface. Scatter the fennel seeds over the dough and knead until the dough comes together, about 1 minute. Evenly divide the dough to form 12 rolls. Shape each roll into a ball. Place the rolls onto the baking sheet, flatten slightly, and, using a sharp knife, cut a shallow X on top of each roll. Bake the rolls until golden and a toothpick inserted in the center comes out clean, about 25 minutes. If not serving hot, place the rolls on a rack to cool.

Makes 12 rolls

Fennel has long been valued in India and Asia as an aid to digestion as well as a condiment. In India, fennel water is used to treat colic in babies.

Marjoram Shallot Butter

Serve this herb-flecked butter on rolls, mashed potatoes, rice, or vegetables. It is also a delightful seasoning to rub under the skin of turkey or chicken before roasting.

8 tablespoons (1 stick) butter, at room temperature
2 tablespoons finely diced shallots
1 teaspoon marjoram
1 tablespoon dry white wine (optional)

Melt 1 tablespoon of the butter in a small skillet over medium heat. Add the shallots and sauté until soft, about 3 minutes. Remove the pan from the heat and set aside to cool.

Combine the remaining 7 tablespoons of butter and the marjoram in a small bowl. Add the shallots and wine, if using, and stir until combined.

Serve the butter immediately. Store leftover butter in an airtight container in the refrigerator.

Makes about ¾ cup

fun fact

At medieval coronations and church ceremonies, marjoram was strewn about the floors to make a fragrant bed that perfumed the air as people walked on it.

Desserts and Sweets

Whether they come as a midafternoon snack, a party treat, or at the end of a satisfying meal, sweets have a way of taking center stage in our food dreams. This collection of recipes shows why. Desserts and sweet treats can take many mouthwatering forms, from a classically elegant crème brûlée to an apple pie bursting with fresh-fruit flavor. We have also included cupcakes, cookies, fruit bars, and even some old-fashioned favorites like a chocolate Texas "sheath cake" and a caramel apple sundae that will make you think you're back at the state fair.

Of course, the fun of these recipes is that they all take the flavor up a notch or two by making use of vibrant, organic spices and herbs, sometimes in unexpected ways. Can lovely crème brûlée get better? Try our cardamom-laced version and we think you'll agree that it can. Do herbs belong in desserts? Taste the thyme in our cornmeal pound cake and the rosemary in our roasted peaches, and you'll be inspired to find other ways to freshen up your favorite sweet treats.

Cardamom Crème Brûlée

Something about crème brûlée's sugary crust on top of a creamy custard is just plain addictive. It's even worth a little extra effort. As much as we love crème brûlée adorned only with vanilla, this cardamom-laced version has won our hearts.

> **4 cups heavy cream**
> **12 egg yolks, beaten**
> **1 cup plus 3 tablespoons sugar**
> **4 teaspoons vanilla**
> **1 teaspoon ground** green cardamom

Preheat the oven to 325°F. Warm the cream in a medium saucepan over medium heat until little bubbles form around the edge of the pan. While the cream is warming, whisk together the eggs and 1 cup of the sugar in a large mixing bowl. Gradually whisk the warmed cream into the egg mixture and continue whisking until the sugar is completely dissolved. Strain the mixture through a fine-mesh sieve into another bowl or large measuring cup. Add the vanilla and cardamom and stir until the mixture is completely combined.

Place 6 crème brûlée ramekins into a large, shallow baking dish. Fill each ramekin to the top with the custard mixture. Pour enough hot water into the baking dish so that the water comes halfway up the sides of the ramekins. Carefully transfer the dish to the oven. Bake until the crème brûlée is just set but still slightly quivery in the center, about 25 minutes. Remove the crème brûlée ramekins from the baking dish and allow them to cool. Cover and refrigerate for at least 2 hours or until ready to serve.

Remove the crème brûlée from the refrigerator and let rest for 30 minutes before serving. Using the remaining sugar, evenly sprinkle 1½ teaspoons of sugar on the surface of each crème brûlée. Using a propane torch, caramelize the sugar by holding the torch 2 inches from the surface of the custard and rotating the custard until the sugar is evenly melted. Serve immediately.

Serves 6

Lemon Thyme Cornmeal Pound Cake

with

Balsamic Basil Berries and Zesty Whipped Cream

We've always found pound cake irresistible, with its simple but seductive formula of butter, sugar, eggs, flour, and maybe a flavoring or two. But ever eager for a new pound cake adventure, we were persuaded to try a cornmeal-flour mixture plus, of course, a couple of spices. Now we're not sure we can go back to the plain old flour-and-vanilla recipe.

The lemon zest brightens the batter, and the thyme adds a pleasant herbal note. This cake is good any time of day and all year-round. When you have access to fresh berries, seize the opportunity to serve this with Balsamic Basil Berries. Top it all with Zesty Whipped Cream for a satisfying and elegant dessert.

16 tablespoons (2 sticks) unsalted butter, at room temperature
1½ cups sugar
5 eggs
1½ teaspoons vanilla
1 cup all-purpose flour
1 cup yellow cornmeal

2 teaspoons dried lemon zest
1 teaspoon thyme
½ teaspoon salt
3 cups Balsamic Basil Berries (recipe follows)
2 cups Zesty Whipped Cream (recipe follows)

Preheat the oven to 325°F and grease a 9 by 5-inch loaf pan. Cream the butter and sugar in a large mixing bowl until light and fluffy. In a medium bowl, whisk together the eggs and vanilla. Add the egg mixture to the butter mixture and beat until combined. Mix together the flour, cornmeal, lemon zest, thyme, and salt in a small bowl. Gradually add the flour mixture to the butter mixture and beat until the batter is combined.

Pour the batter into the prepared pan and bake until a toothpick inserted in the center of the cake comes out clean, 60 to 70 minutes. Allow the cake to cool in the pan for 10 minutes, then remove it from the pan and place on a rack to cool before slicing. Serve the pound cake topped with balsamic basil berries and whipped cream.

Variations: Use orange zest instead of lemon zest in both the cornmeal pound cake and zesty whipped cream recipes, and substitute rosemary for the thyme in the pound cake.

Serves 8 to 10

During the Middle Ages, people put thyme under their pillows to ward off nightmares.

Balsamic Basil Berries

Basil and balsamic vinegar are perfect counterpoints to the sweet-tart summer flavors of ripe strawberries. Be sure to use a good-quality balsamic vinegar.

1 (16-ounce) container strawberries, hulled and quartered
1½ teaspoons sugar
1 teaspoon balsamic vinegar
1 teaspoon basil

Gently toss the strawberries with the sugar, vinegar, and basil in a medium bowl. Let the strawberries sit at room temperature until they release their juices, about 30 minutes but no longer than 90 minutes.

Makes 3 cups

Zesty Whipped Cream

Zest pairs beautifully with cream. This recipe is equally good with orange zest.

1 cup cold heavy whipping cream
¼ cup sifted confectioners' sugar
1 teaspoon dried lemon zest
½ teaspoon vanilla

Beat the cream on medium speed in a chilled mixing bowl with chilled beaters until thickened. Stir in the sugar, lemon zest, and vanilla and continue beating on medium speed until soft peaks form. Perfectly whipped cream should be billowy and stiff but still smooth. Serve the whipped cream immediately.

Makes 2 to 2½ cups

Roasted Peaches

 with

Rosemary Streusel and Cinnamon Whipped Cream

When fresh peaches arrive in markets or at roadside stands, you know it's time to feast on fruit. Like Aunt Sara in Alabama, we can eat them morning, noon, and night. Here's an easy but elegant peach dessert.

4 tablespoons (½ stick) butter, melted
2 tablespoons sugar
2 tablespoons firmly packed brown sugar
1 teaspoon rosemary
1 teaspoon ground cinnamon
½ teaspoon ground ginger
¼ teaspoon vanilla
⅛ teaspoon salt
¾ cup all-purpose flour
4 medium peaches, halved and pitted
Cinnamon Whipped Cream, for topping (recipe follows)

Preheat the oven to 425°F and grease an 8-inch square or round baking pan. Whisk together the butter, sugar, brown sugar, rosemary, cinnamon, ginger, vanilla, and salt in a medium bowl. Add the flour and stir with a wooden spoon until the streusel comes together and is crumbly.

Arrange the peach halves, cut side up, in the prepared pan. Top the peaches with equal amounts of streusel. Roast until the peaches are tender and the streusel is browned, about 20 minutes. Cover the peaches with aluminum foil if they are browning too quickly. Serve the peaches warm topped with cinnamon whipped cream.

Serves 4

Cinnamon Whipped Cream

A touch of cinnamon is a delightful way to spice up whipped cream.

> **1 cup cold heavy whipping cream**
> **¼ cup sifted confectioners' sugar**
> **½ teaspoon vanilla**
> **¼ to ½ teaspoon ground cinnamon**

Beat the cream on medium speed in a chilled mixing bowl with chilled beaters until thickened. Stir in the sugar, vanilla, and cinnamon and continue beating on medium speed until soft peaks form. Perfectly whipped cream should be billowy and stiff but still smooth. Serve the whipped cream immediately.

Makes 2 to 2½ cups

fun fact

Cinnamon was so valuable in ancient Rome that a pound of cinnamon oil cost as much as a centurion could earn in six years. Ancient Romans wooed barbarian chieftains with diplomatic gifts of spices like pepper, cassia, and cinnamon.

Fresh Apple Streusel Cake

Here's a great way to enjoy fresh apples, a streusel cake made even more tempting by the gentle touch of coriander and cinnamon. Granny Smith or other tart apples are best. This treat is equally good warm from the oven or served later at room temperature. Either way, you'll find it hard to settle for just one piece.

Streusel Topping

½ cup all-purpose flour
½ cup sugar
½ cup firmly packed brown sugar
1 teaspoon organic ground coriander
4 tablespoons (½ stick) butter, at room temperature

Cake

1 cup sugar
¾ cup vegetable oil
1 egg
1 teaspoon vanilla
1½ cups all-purpose flour
2 teaspoons ground coriander
1 teaspoon ground cinnamon
½ teaspoon baking powder
½ teaspoon baking soda
½ teaspoon salt
2 cups peeled, diced apples
1 cup chopped walnuts

Preheat the oven to 350°F and grease and flour an 8-inch square or round baking pan. To make the streusel topping, combine the flour, sugar, brown sugar, and coriander in a medium bowl. Cut in the butter with a pastry blender or two knives until the mixture is crumbly. Set the streusel topping aside.

To make the cake, beat the sugar, oil, egg, and vanilla together on medium speed in a large bowl. Sift the flour, coriander, cinnamon, baking powder, baking soda, and salt into a small bowl. Gradually add the flour mixture to the batter and beat until well mixed. Stir in the apples and walnuts.

Pour the batter into the prepared pan. Evenly sprinkle the streusel topping over the cake batter. Bake the cake for 40 minutes, or until a toothpick inserted in the center comes out clean.

Makes 1 (8-inch square or round) cake

Spice traders in colonial Connecticut conned their customers by whittling counterfeit "nutmegs" from ordinary wood. That's why Connecticut's nickname is "the nutmeg state."

Patty's Apple Pie

We thought we knew how good apple pie could be. Then we tasted apple pie made by Patty Oakley Audia, at Atwater's in Baltimore, our favorite bakery and soup bar. When Patty offered to share her recipe with us, we eagerly accepted.

Patty says the secret to a good apple pie is to use a variety of fresh, local apples. The different flavors will enhance one another. Another secret, of course, is to use fresh-tasting, organic spices. Use our Basic Pie Crust Dough (page 169), with a teaspoon of cardamom or allspice to complement the apple filling.

> **3 pounds apples (any variety), peeled and cored**
> **2 tablespoons lemon juice**
> **2 teaspoons dried** lemon zest
> **½ cup sugar**
> **¼ cup firmly packed brown sugar**
> **1 teaspoon ground** true cinnamon
> **1 teaspoon ground** nutmeg
> **½ cup all-purpose flour**
> **Double recipe Basic Pie Crust Dough (page 169)**
> **Whole milk and sugar, for finishing**

Preheat the oven to 375°F and grease a 9-inch deep-dish pie plate. To make the filling, cut the apples into ½-inch-thick slices and place in a large bowl. Add the lemon juice, lemon zest, sugar, brown sugar, cinnamon, and nutmeg and toss well. Add the flour and toss again.

Roll the pie dough on a floured surface and transfer to the prepared pie plate. The dough should be big enough to hang over the edges of the pie plate. Mound in the filling. Roll out the remaining pie dough so it is large enough to cover the top of the pie just to the edges of the dish. Roll the bottom crust up around the dish edge, catching the top crust in the roll. (This is a learned skill, so be patient.)

Score the crust as you wish, using a knife to make slits for steam to escape. Brush the crust with whole milk and sprinkle with sugar. Bake for 1 hour, or until the bubbles are thick and the crust is nicely browned.

Makes 1 (9-inch) deep-dish pie

fun fact

Medieval Viagra? An eleventh-century treatise on sex, written by a monk, recommends a concoction of cinnamon, ginger, and herbs to be taken after meals as a cure for impotence. If the impotence was only occasional, honey and chickpeas could be added to the recipe.

Basic Pie Crust Dough

Why waste a chance to spice things up? This basic recipe for pie crust dough will come in handy in many ways—from potpies to quiches to apple pies. There's no reason to settle for plain old dough when a teaspoon of this or that will add alluring accents to your finished dish. Master this dough, and give some thought to how to spice (or herb) it up, and you'll soon feel like a flavor artist at work.

1½ cups all-purpose flour
1½ tablespoons sugar
1 teaspoon spice (such as basil, coriander, cloves, ginger, or a combination)
½ teaspoon salt
8 tablespoons (1 stick) chilled unsalted butter, cut into small pieces
1 egg yolk, beaten
2 tablespoons ice water

Combine the flour, sugar, spice, and salt in a medium bowl. Cut in the butter with a pastry blender or two knives until the butter is evenly distributed in the flour mixture and the mixture is crumbly. Gently cut in the egg yolk and enough of the 2 tablespoons of ice water to make the dough just hold together. Add more ice water if necessary. Shape the dough into a round, flat disk, wrap tightly in plastic wrap, and refrigerate for at least 30 minutes.

Lightly flour the work surface. Roll the chilled dough from the center out in all directions until the dough is ⅛ inch thick and 3 to 4 inches wider than the pie plate. Transfer the dough to the pie plate, trim the edges, and finish as desired.

Makes 1 (9-inch) pie crust

Pumpkin Cream Cheese Pie  Ginger Crust

If you don't have a favorite pumpkin pie recipe—or even if you do—here's a version that will convince you that pumpkin should not be restricted to Thanksgiving feasts. Pumpkin is loaded with vitamins, and with canned pumpkin readily available, this is a pie your family and friends will love any time of year.

Crust

1¼ cups graham cracker crumbs
8 tablespoons (1 stick) butter, melted
3 tablespoons sugar
1 teaspoon ground ginger

Filling

2 (8-ounce) packages cream cheese, at
    room temperature
1 cup sugar
2 eggs
1 teaspoon vanilla
½ cup canned pumpkin
1 teaspoon ground cinnamon
1 teaspoon ground allspice

Topping

¾ cup chopped pecans
¼ cup firmly packed brown sugar
2 tablespoons butter, at room
    temperature

Whipped cream, for garnish

Preheat the oven to 350°F. To make the crust, mix the graham cracker crumbs, butter, 3 tablespoons of sugar, and ginger in a small bowl. Press the crust mixture into the bottom and up the sides of a 9-inch pie plate.

To make the filling, beat together the cream cheese and 1 cup of sugar in a large mixing bowl until smooth and creamy. In a small bowl, whisk together the eggs and vanilla. Slowly add the egg mixture to the cream cheese mixture and beat until smooth and creamy. Measure out and reserve 1 cup of the cream cheese mixture. Pour the remaining cream cheese mixture into the pie crust.

In a medium bowl, mix the pumpkin, cinnamon, allspice, and the reserved cream cheese mixture. Carefully pour and spread the pumpkin mixture over the cream cheese filling. Bake for 30 minutes. While the pie is baking, combine the pecans, brown sugar, and butter in a small bowl.

Remove the pie from the oven and cover the edges with aluminum foil or a pie crust shield. Sprinkle the pecan mixture over the top of the pie and bake for an additional 10 minutes. Allow the pie to cool for 1 to 2 hours and then refrigerate for at least 3 hours before serving. Serve with whipped cream.

Makes 1 (9-inch) pie

Pumpkin Spice–Chocolate Chip Muffins

We love spice-friendly pumpkin in bread and muffins, and we consider chocolate an essential food. But we don't often see these two great flavors in the same recipe, and that's why we love these spicy muffins. We think you'll agree that pumpkin, spices, and chocolate make a tasty trio. Perfect for fall celebrations, they'll be equally welcome the rest of the year.

1½ cups all-purpose flour

1 teaspoon plus 1 teaspoon ground cinnamon

1 teaspoon ground allspice

1 teaspoon baking powder

½ teaspoon baking soda

½ teaspoon salt

1¼ cups plus 2 tablespoons sugar

1 (15-ounce) can pumpkin

⅓ cup vegetable oil

2 eggs

1 teaspoon vanilla

1 cup semisweet chocolate chips

Preheat the oven to 350°F and grease 18 standard-size muffin cups or line them with 18 paper cups. Sift the flour, 1 teaspoon of the cinnamon, allspice, baking powder, baking soda, and salt into a large mixing bowl. In a medium mixing bowl, whisk 1¼ cups of the sugar together with the pumpkin, oil, eggs, and vanilla. Stir the chocolate chips into the pumpkin mixture. Add the pumpkin mixture to the flour mixture and mix until the batter just comes together. Stir the remaining 2 tablespoons of sugar and the remaining 1 teaspoon of cinnamon together in a small bowl.

Spoon ⅓ cup of the batter into each of the prepared muffin cups. Sprinkle the cinnamon sugar mixture evenly over the top of each muffin. Bake the muffins until a toothpick inserted in the center of one or two muffins comes out clean, 25 to 30 minutes. Remove the muffins from the oven and allow them to cool for 5 minutes before removing them from the pan. If not serving the muffins hot, place the muffins on a rack to cool.

Makes 18 muffins

On their bitter retreat from Moscow, Napoleon's troops are said to have warmed their feet by placing allspice in their boots.

Gingerbread Cupcakes Cardamom Cream Cheese Frosting

Next time your kids mention gingerbread, surprise them with these cupcakes. Better yet, let them help you make them. Molasses and brown sugar form a rich flavor stage for some of our favorite spices to dance on. You'll be tempted to eat these cupcakes right out of the oven, but take our word for it—the Cardamom Cream Cheese Frosting is worth the wait.

8 tablespoons (1 stick) unsalted butter, at room temperature
½ cup firmly packed brown sugar
½ cup molasses
1 egg
½ teaspoon vanilla
½ cup boiling water
1 teaspoon baking soda

1½ cups all-purpose flour
2 teaspoons ground cinnamon
1 teaspoon ground ginger
1 teaspoon ground cloves
1 teaspoon dried lemon zest
¼ teaspoon salt
1⅓ cups Cardamom Cream Cheese Frosting (recipe follows)

Preheat the oven to 350°F and grease 12 standard-size muffin cups or line them with paper cups. Cream the butter and brown sugar in a large mixing bowl until light and fluffy. Beat in the molasses, egg, and vanilla. In a small bowl, stir together the boiling water and baking soda until dissolved. Stir the baking soda water into the molasses mixture.

Sift together the flour, cinnamon, ginger, cloves, lemon zest, and salt into a small bowl. Whisk the flour mixture into the molasses mixture until the batter is combined.

Spoon the batter into the prepared muffin cups. Bake the cupcakes until a toothpick inserted in the center of one or two of the cupcakes comes out clean, about 20 minutes. Remove the cupcakes from the oven and allow them to cool for 5 minutes before removing them from the pan. Place the cupcakes on a rack to cool for 30 minutes. Spread the cream cheese frosting generously over the cooled cupcakes.

Makes 12 cupcakes

Ancient Chinese courtiers chewed cloves to freshen their breath before audiences with the emperor.

Cardamom Cream Cheese Frosting

This frosting is simple to make and easy to love. It's sensational on the gingerbread cupcakes, but you'll find plenty of other ways to use this recipe. Feel free to adjust the spice to your own preference. Orange zest would be a nice substitute for the lemon. We're always partial to cardamom, the Queen of Spices, but allspice or cinnamon would work well, too.

8 ounces cream cheese, at room temperature
1½ cups confectioners' sugar
½ teaspoon vanilla
1 tablespoon fresh lemon juice
2 teaspoons dried lemon zest
1 teaspoon ground green cardamom

Cream together the cream cheese and sugar in a medium mixing bowl until light and fluffy. Beat in the vanilla. Add the lemon juice, lemon zest, and cardamom and beat until fluffy and smooth. Chill the frosting in the refrigerator until ready to use.

Makes 1⅓ cups

Pear Cream Cheese Bars Macadamia Nut Crust

These creamy bars are fun to make and they will be quick to disappear. They are perfect for dessert, for a party, or for an after-school treat. Our favorite variation: omit the cloves in the crust and use 1 teaspoon organic thyme instead.

Crust

4 tablespoons (½ stick) butter, softened
¼ cup sugar
½ cup all-purpose flour
1 teaspoon ground ginger
1 teaspoon ground cloves
½ cup macadamia nuts, finely chopped

Filling

12 ounces cream cheese, at room temperature
¾ cup sugar
1 egg
½ teaspoon vanilla
2 pears, peeled, cored, and sliced

Streusel Topping

½ cup all-purpose flour
¼ cup firmly packed brown sugar
1 teaspoon ground cinnamon
1 teaspoon ground coriander
4 tablespoons (½ stick) cold butter, cut into small pieces
½ cup macadamia nuts, chopped

Preheat the oven to 350°F and grease an 8-inch square or round baking pan. To make the crust, cream the butter and sugar in a medium bowl until light and fluffy. Gradually beat in the flour, ginger, and cloves. Stir in the macadamia nuts. Press the crust mixture into the bottom of the pan and bake for 15 minutes.

Increase the oven temperature to 375°F. To make the filling, beat together the cream cheese and sugar in a large mixing bowl until smooth and creamy. In a small bowl, whisk together the egg and vanilla. Slowly add the egg mixture to the cream cheese mixture and beat until smooth and creamy. Spread the cream cheese mixture over the crust. Arrange the pears on top of the cream cheese mixture.

To make the streusel topping, combine the flour, brown sugar, cinnamon, and coriander in a small bowl. Cut in the butter with a pastry blender or two knives until the butter is evenly distributed in the flour mixture and the mixture is crumbly. Stir in the macadamia nuts. Evenly sprinkle the streusel topping over the pears. Bake the bars for 25 to 30 minutes. Allow the bars to cool and then refrigerate for at least 3 hours before cutting and serving.

Makes 12 bars

Sweet Heat Brownies

. . . .

Chocolate is one of our favorite backdrops for spices, and this chile-cinnamon brownie shows why. At a promotion for **tsp spices**, the store's bakers prepared a couple of trays of these brownies. Now the "**tsp spices** Sweet Heat Brownie" is a regular item there.

You should give some thought to how much chile pepper you want in the brownie. We have made this recipe with as many as 6 teaspoons of chile, but that provides quite a kick. For most people, 4 teaspoons will provide a distinct but not overpowering tingle. If you're not sure what your heat tolerance is for chile peppers, you may want to start with 3 teaspoons. The orange zest and dates add a mellow richness, tying all the flavors together.

4 ounces good-quality unsweetened chocolate

8 tablespoons (1 stick) butter

3 large eggs

1½ cups sugar

1 teaspoon vanilla

3 to 4 teaspoons ground ancho chile pepper **(more, if you like it spicier)**

1 teaspoon dried orange zest

2 teaspoons ground cinnamon

½ cup all-purpose flour

¼ teaspoon salt

1 cup dried dates, roughly chopped

1 cup chopped pecans

¼ cup salted, toasted pumpkin seeds

Preheat the oven to 350°F. Grease an 8 by 12-inch baking pan and set aside.

Melt the chocolate and butter together in the top of a double boiler or carefully in the microwave. Let it cool a bit.

Meanwhile, with an electric mixer, beat together the eggs, sugar, vanilla, ancho chile, orange zest, and cinnamon. Stir the chocolate-butter mixture into the egg mixture, then stir in the flour, salt, and dates. Reserve a handful of pecans and pumpkin seeds to sprinkle on top before baking, then stir in the rest of the pecans and pumpkin seeds.

Spoon the mixture into the pan and spread evenly. Bake until the center is just set, about 25 minutes, checking to be sure the edges are not burning. Do not overbake, or the brownies will lose their chewy texture.

Let cool in the pan for at least 30 minutes before cutting.

Makes about 24 (2 by 2-inch) brownies

Coco's Chocolate Sheath Cake

We're not exactly sure why this is called a "sheath cake" and not a "sheet cake." But that's what Katie's grandmother Coco called it, and that's good enough for us. Whatever the name, this cake is a multigenerational crowd-pleaser.

We've spiced it up a bit. The chile pepper in the icing is just enough to tickle the tongue. Together with the cinnamon, it creates one of our favorite "sweet heat" spice combinations.

Cake

2 cups all-purpose flour
2 cups sugar
2 teaspoons ground cinnamon
1 teaspoon baking soda
1 cup water
8 tablespoons (1 stick) butter
½ cup vegetable oil
¼ cup unsweetened cocoa powder
½ cup buttermilk
2 eggs
1 teaspoon vanilla

Icing

8 tablespoons (1 stick) butter
6 tablespoons milk
¼ cup unsweetened cocoa powder
1 teaspoon vanilla
1 teaspoon ground cinnamon
1 teaspoon ground ancho chile pepper **or** mild chile pepper
1 (1-pound) box confectioners' sugar, sifted
1 cup chopped pecans

Preheat the oven to 400°F and grease and flour a 13 by 9 by 2-inch cake pan. Sift the flour, sugar, cinnamon, and baking soda into a large mixing bowl. Combine the water, butter, oil, and cocoa powder in a medium saucepan and bring to a boil over high heat, whisking continually. Pour the boiling cocoa mixture over the flour mixture and mix until combined. In a small bowl, whisk together the buttermilk, eggs, and vanilla. Add the egg mixture to the chocolate batter and mix well.

Pour the batter into the prepared pan and bake until a toothpick inserted in the center of the cake comes out clean, about 20 minutes. Five minutes before the cake is done, begin making the icing.

To make the icing, combine the butter, milk, cocoa powder, vanilla, cinnamon, and chile pepper in a medium saucepan. Bring to a boil over high heat, whisking continually. Remove the saucepan from the heat and stir in the confectioners' sugar and pecans. Spread the chocolate icing evenly over the hot chocolate cake.

Makes 1 (13 by 9 by 2-inch) cake

Oatmeal–Chocolate Chip Walnut Cookies

When our friend Camille first shared a version of this recipe with us, she called it "The World's Best Cookie." It was pretty darn good, but in our view there's not much out there that spices can't improve. We added some, and the world's best cookie got even better.

16 tablespoons (2 sticks) unsalted butter, at room temperature
1 cup firmly packed brown sugar
1 cup sugar
2 eggs
2 tablespoons whole milk
2 teaspoons vanilla
2 cups all-purpose flour

1 teaspoon ground cinnamon
1 teaspoon ground cloves
1 teaspoon salt
1 teaspoon baking powder
1 teaspoon baking soda
2½ cups old-fashioned rolled oats
2 cups semisweet chocolate chips
1½ cups chopped walnuts

Preheat the oven to 350°F. Cream the butter, brown sugar, and sugar in a large mixing bowl until light and fluffy. In a small bowl, whisk together the eggs, milk, and vanilla. Add the egg mixture to the butter mixture and beat until combined.

Sift the flour, cinnamon, cloves, salt, baking powder, and baking soda into a medium bowl. Gradually add the flour mixture to the butter mixture and beat until combined. Stir in the oats, chocolate chips, and walnuts. Drop the cookie dough by rounded tablespoons onto an ungreased baking sheet. Bake the cookies for 10 to 12 minutes, or until the centers are set. Remove the cookies from the oven and allow them to cool for 2 minutes before removing them from the baking sheet.

Makes about 2½ dozen cookies

Variation: Substitute 1 teaspoon ground cardamom for the cloves.

French adventurer Pierre Poivre hatched his plan to smuggle clove and nutmeg seedlings from the Dutch-controlled Moluccas in 1745, but it took him 25 years to succeed. Descendants of some of the original clove trees he obtained in 1770 still grow in the former royal garden on the Île-de-France in Paris.

Bittersweet Chocolate Chip–Ginger Cookies

These chocolate morsels are rich and gooey when they're warm. When cool, the spice flavors turn a chocolate cookie into a transcendental flavor trip. You'll be hard-pressed to love a plain chocolate cookie ever again.

12 tablespoons (1½ sticks) unsalted butter, at room temperature
1 cup firmly packed brown sugar
1 egg
1 teaspoon vanilla
¼ cup molasses
2 cups all-purpose flour
⅓ cup unsweetened cocoa powder
2 teaspoons baking soda
2 teaspoons ground ginger
1 teaspoon ground cinnamon
1 teaspoon ground cloves
1 teaspoon ground nutmeg
½ teaspoon salt
1½ cups bittersweet chocolate chips
Confectioners' sugar, for rolling

Cream the butter and brown sugar in a large mixing bowl until light and fluffy. In a small bowl, whisk together the egg and vanilla. Add the egg mixture and the molasses into the butter mixture and beat until combined.

Sift the flour, cocoa powder, baking soda, ginger, cinnamon, cloves, nutmeg, and salt into a medium bowl. Gradually add the flour mixture to the butter mixture and beat until combined. Stir in the chocolate chips. Cover the dough and chill for at least 2 hours.

Preheat the oven to 350°F. Scoop the cookie dough by rounded tablespoons and roll into balls. Roll each ball in confectioners' sugar until well coated and place onto an ungreased baking sheet. Bake the cookies for 12 to 14 minutes, or until the centers are set. Remove the cookies from the oven and allow them to cool for 2 minutes before removing them from the baking sheet.

Makes about 3 dozen cookies

fun facts

One Arabic medical text recommended mixing ginger with honey and rubbing it in strategic places on the man's body to treat a lackluster love life. In India, ginger paste is applied to the temples as a headache remedy.

The price of nutmeg skyrocketed in Elizabethan London when physicians claimed that their nutmeg pomanders could cure the plague.

Spiced Caramel Sauce

Cloves add a spicy note to this mellow caramel sauce. Use it with Caramel Apple Sundaes (page 182), or use it as a topping for vanilla ice cream. For a variation, substitute cinnamon, allspice, or ginger for the cloves.

1 cup heavy cream
1¼ cups firmly packed brown sugar
1 teaspoon ground cloves
4 tablespoons (½ stick) butter
1 teaspoon vanilla

Bring the cream to a boil in a small saucepan over medium heat. Add the brown sugar and cloves and cook, stirring continually, until the sugar dissolves, about 5 minutes. Remove the saucepan from the heat and whisk in the butter 1 tablespoon at a time. Stir in the vanilla and serve immediately.

Makes 2 cups

Caramel Apple Sundaes

• •

Do you remember your first caramel apple, the joy of encountering that enchanting combination of the sweet crunch of the apple against the buttery smoothness of the caramel coating? This recipe creates the caramel apple in the form of an ice-cream sundae. This time, it's a treat for all ages.

4 small Granny Smith apples, cored and cut into 6 slices
1 pint vanilla ice cream
2 cups Spiced Caramel Sauce, warmed (page 181)
Whipped Cream, for topping
½ cup Cardamom Candied Walnuts (page 79),
   roughly chopped
4 strawberries, sliced and fanned, for garnish

Arrange 6 apple slices into a ring in each of 4 individual serving bowls. Place a scoop of ice cream in the center of each apple ring. Spoon ½ cup of the spiced caramel sauce over each ice-cream sundae. Top with whipped cream and cardamom candied walnuts, roughly chopped. Garnish the top of each sundae with a strawberry. Serve the sundaes immediately.

Serves 4

Metric Conversions and Equivalents

Metric Conversion Formulas

To Convert	Multiply
Ounces to grams	Ounces by 28.35
Pounds to kilograms	Pounds by .454
Teaspoons to milliliters	Teaspoons by 4.93
Tablespoons to milliliters	Tablespoons by 14.79
Fluid ounces to milliliters	Fluid ounces by 29.57
Cups to milliliters	Cups by 236.59
Cups to liters	Cups by .236
Pints to liters	Pints by .473
Quarts to liters	Quarts by .946
Gallons to liters	Gallons by 3.785
Inches to centimeters	Inches by 2.54

Approximate Metric Equivalents

Weight

¼ ounce	7 grams
½ ounce	14 grams
¾ ounce	21 grams
1 ounce	28 grams
1¼ ounces	35 grams
1½ ounces	42.5 grams
1⅔ ounces	45 grams
2 ounces	57 grams
3 ounces	85 grams
4 ounces (¼ pound)	113 grams
5 ounces	142 grams
6 ounces	170 grams
7 ounces	198 grams
8 ounces (½ pound)	227 grams
16 ounces (1 pound)	454 grams
35.25 ounces (2.2 pounds)	1 kilogram

Length

⅛ inch	3 millimeters
¼ inch	6 millimeters
½ inch	1¼ centimeters
1 inch	2½ centimeters
2 inches	5 centimeters
2½ inches	6 centimeters
4 inches	10 centimeters
5 inches	13 centimeters
6 inches	15¼ centimeters
12 inches (1 foot)	30 centimeters

Volume

¼ teaspoon	1 milliliter
½ teaspoon	2.5 milliliters
¾ teaspoon	4 milliliters
1 teaspoon	5 milliliters
1¼ teaspoons	6 milliliters
1½ teaspoons	7.5 milliliters
1¾ teaspoons	8.5 milliliters
2 teaspoons	10 milliliters
1 tablespoon (½ fluid ounce)	15 milliliters
2 tablespoons (1 fluid ounce)	30 milliliters
¼ cup	60 milliliters
⅓ cup	80 milliliters
½ cup (4 fluid ounces)	120 milliliters
⅓ cup	160 milliliters
¾ cup	180 milliliters
1 cup (8 fluid ounces)	240 milliliters
1¼ cups	300 milliliters
1½ cups (12 fluid ounces)	360 milliliters
1⅔ cups	400 milliliters
2 cups (1 pint)	460 milliliters
3 cups	700 milliliters
4 cups (1 quart)	0.95 liter
1 quart plus ¼ cup	1 liter
4 quarts (1 gallon)	3.8 liters

Oven Temperatures

To convert Fahrenheit to Celsius, subtract 32 from Fahrenheit, multiply the result by 5, then divide by 9.

Description	Fahrenheit	Celsius	British Gas Mark
Very cool	200°	95°	0
Very cool	225°	110°	¼
Very cool	250°	120°	½
Cool	275°	135°	1
Cool	300°	150°	2
Warm	325°	165°	3
Moderate	350°	175°	4
Moderately hot	375°	190°	5
Fairly hot	400°	200°	6
Hot	425°	220°	7
Very hot	450°	230°	8
Very hot	475°	245°	9

Common Ingredients and Their Approximate Equivalents

1 cup uncooked white rice = 185 grams

1 cup all-purpose flour = 140 grams

1 stick butter (4 ounces • ½ cup • 8 tablespoons) = 110 grams

1 cup butter (8 ounces • 2 sticks • 16 tablespoons) = 220 grams

1 cup brown sugar, firmly packed = 225 grams

1 cup granulated sugar = 200 grams

Information compiled from a variety of sources, including *Recipes into Type* by Joan Whitman and Dolores Simon (Newton, MA: Biscuit Books, 2000); *The New Food Lover's Companion* by Sharon Tyler Herbst (Hauppauge, NY: Barron's, 1995); and *Rosemary Brown's Big Kitchen Instruction Book* (Kansas City, MO: Andrews McMeel, 1998).

Index